P9-DND-551

# Unicorns Are Real

## A Right-Brained Approach to Learning

by Barbara Meister Vitale

WARNER BOOKS

A Warner Communications Company

WARNER BOOKS EDITION

This Warner Books Edition is published by arrangement with
Jalmar Press, 45 Hitching Post Drive, Building 2, Rolling Hills
Estates, California 90274.

Artwork by Jacqueline Lamer Lockwood
Text design by Nicola Mazzella

Warner Books, Inc.
666 Fifth Avenue
New York, N.Y. 10103

 A Warner Communications Company

Printed in the United States of America

First Warner Books Printing: February, 1986

10 9 8 7 6 5 4 3 2 1

*"I strongly feel that the insight gained from **Unicorns** would prove invaluable to educators and enable them to give all children equal access to learning."*

**—Rose Marie Swanson,**
Office of Instructional Improvement,
Detroit Public Schools

*       *       *

**BARBARA MEISTER VITALE** was a child with learning disabilities. Thanks to two teachers who recognized and encouraged her creative abilities, she was able to complete high school and later earn a bachelor's degree in education, a master's degree in early childhood and learning disabilities, and a specialist degree in administration and supervision.

Mrs. Vitale has taught students of all levels, from kindergarten to college, from gifted to autistic, from learning disabled to emotionally disturbed. She has trained teachers in curriculum and instructional strategies for normal and special needs in the elementary grades. Presently a full-time author and lecturer, Mrs. Vitale has spoken to such groups as The International Association for Children with Learning Disabilities, The Association of American School Administrators, The Association for the Advancement of Children and Adults with Learning Disabilities, and The International Society of Accelerative Learning and Teaching. She is recognized as an expert on the implications of brain research on children's education.

TO


My teachers—who believed in me

Mrs. Walter Grosh
and
Mrs. Evelyn Brunner


My Grandmother—who taught me to love

Fanny McNeil


And
to
GOD

# ACKNOWLEDGMENTS

I wish to thank all my friends and co-workers who believe in Unicorns.

Special thanks go to Joan McCabe, who corrected my spelling and grammar, Sharon Kaidor, who typed the manuscript more times than she cares to remember, Suzanne Mikesell, my editor, Ron Brandt, for being a friend and for playing the devil's advocate, and Louis Vitale, who survived it all.

I am especially grateful to:

Palm Beach County School system
Dr. William Drainer
William Myers
Dr. Phil Dagostino
Dr. Sylvia Richardson
Dr. Ronald Cantwell
Greater Cincinnati Association for Children with Learning Disabilities (ACLD)
Unity Elementary School, West Palm Beach, Florida

# PREFACE

There are many children who do not learn in school or who experience difficulties understanding new concepts as they are introduced in school. As their parents and teachers, we should interpret their disinterest, confusion, or lack of comprehension as signals that the methods we have been using, for whatever reasons, just are not working. We must ask, "Why isn't the material reaching the student?" rather than "Why isn't the student grasping the material?" There's a big difference in the way we formulate the problem: in the first case, we are treating the student as the problem; in the second, the method is the problem.

Barbara Meister Vitale honors each learner with respect and dignity. In UNICORNS ARE REAL she helps us to trust the inner workings of every mind, young or old. If you are a parent, a teacher, or a student of any new subject matter, you will find encouragement from her approach. You have within what it takes to succeed. If you experience difficulty in your search, it just might be that the instructional method has not yet provided what you need in order to integrate or create ideas, to achieve mastery of the new skill.

Everyone, of course, has right and left hemisphere capabilities and modes of consciousness. They work together in an extremely coordinated way. Both are needed for true learning to take place. The left brain organizes and structures information; the right brain creates ideas. The author, nevertheless, feels that schools today have an overabundance of left-brain methods, resulting in the handicapping of those with right-brain or holistic strengths. UNICORNS ARE REAL serves to rectify that imbalance in a unique way.

—The Publisher

# TABLE OF CONTENTS

*Imagination*
*is the unicorn*
*that lifts us above the*
*mundane chains*
*that bind the minds of many*
*and flies us on fantastic wings*
*to a place where dreams DO come true.*

Poem by V. Bassett

# INTRODUCTION

I was a child with a learning disability, labeled "slow" for my first four years at school. I was unable to read until I was twelve years old. Even today I have severe language reversals.

Recently I called a store and asked for the "cycle-bike" department. Luckily, the operator understood my reversal and I bought a bright red three-speed.

If something I write looks backward to you, don't worry about it. I probably wrote it that way. And if the configuration looks weird and the words don't seem to fit together, don't worry about that either. Sometimes the wrong words just sneak into what I'm writing.

I also see everything double and reverse continually, although I don't even realize that I'm doing it. I can't spell either, so you are to ignore all spelling errors in the book—unless, of course, my editor has corrected them.

Other than the above problems, I'm fine. I really am.

I was lucky! When I was in the fifth grade, a wonderful teacher found me and believed in me. She helped me believe in myself! She taught me that my way of thinking was not just different but special! And she taught me to read! She didn't hand me a reading book or instruct me in a reading group; instead, she let me pick out my own books. I picked *Grimm's Fairy Tales*. They were too hard but she never let me know it. We learned the words one by one until I could read a whole story. She also had me make a scrapbook of the one place in the world I would most like to visit. I still remember that scrapbook. I chose Washington State with its magnificent mountains and lush valleys. I learned to read the words under every picture in the scrapbook. I still remember the JOY!

Later, during my high school years, my English teacher helped me find my creative skills and more of myself. She encouraged my writing and accepted my poetry and stories without criticizing the spelling. She didn't even laugh when I proudly stood in front of my literature class and give a report on "ANON," the abbreviation for anonymous, as my favorite author.

Many educators and medical specialists agree that learning problems may be hereditary. I can testify to the hereditary nature of my learning problems. Both of my children have them. My daughter, now 23, still doesn't know left from right. I gave her directions to the beach one day, perhaps five miles from my house, and she wound up almost in the middle of the state. My son is hyperactive, gifted, the "put-Mother-on-the-ceiling" type child with many allergies. He's 20 now and still putting Mother on the ceiling.

Having suffered through learning problems

as a child and as a parent, I know how much it hurts kids to sit there and not learn.

Within the last few years, some have called these children Alpha children, right-brained and creatively different. Recent research on the development and specialization of the brain has opened new doors to understanding how some children learn. Many believe that the research on lateralization and specialization of the hemispheres has important implications for changes in the way we treat children both at home and at school.

Much of today's education continues to be dominated by a left-brained curriculum. As medical research has uncovered more knowledge about the brain and we have begun to understand its implications for our children, small changes are occurring. Parents are asking questions, both parents and teachers are attending seminars and a few school systems are incorporating new ideas into their curriculums. Although this is exciting, a real problem still exists. Most colleges are left-brained in their approach to education and turn out teachers with the same approach. Many talented intuitive teachers leave the field for "greener grass." Those who do stay often find it easier to give in to the system than to fight it. Further, today's parents have come out of this same educational system. Many do not understand their own children.

When libraries are full of technical books

written on the subject of hemispheric special-ization, I feel teachers and parents will benefit from having the information restated in terms of the academic skills children must master in order to be successful in our educational sys-tem. I believe we ought to look at the research in terms of what it tells us about how children learn, rather than why they cannot learn. It is important to understand that children process information and learn in a variety of ways. I believe that by examining hemispheric special-ization and dominance and by identifying indi-vidual thinking patterns, we can find teaching methods that will meet each child's needs.

Although the real problem encompases the entire educational system, we cannot use this as an excuse for not meeting children's needs. The responsibility for providing right-brained experiences lies with both parent and teacher. By being open to and aware of both right- and left-brained consciousness, we can learn to re-spect those capabilities that flow from the non-verbal hemisphere.

Children can be encouraged to explore differ-ent methods of learning. As parents and teach-ers, we can learn with them.

*"A theory is a theory, not a reality. All a theory can do is remind me of certain thoughts that were a part of my reality then."*
—*Hugh Prather*

# 1
# Hemispheric Specialization

An apparently simple organ, the brain is in fact more sophisticated than the most complicated computer. The brain weighs about three pounds. It is composed of two hemispheres, left and right, which are connected by the corpus callosum. The corpus callosum, actually a bundle of nerve tissue, integrates the operations of the two hemispheres (Figure 1). It provides communication between them and allows the transmission of memory and learning.

On visual inspection, the hemispheres appear to be organized bilaterally symmetrical—that is, the right and left sides of the brain look like mirror images of each other. However, they also are organized asymmetrically, meaning there are structural and functional differences between them.

The motor cortex runs along the top of the head on both sides of the brain. It is organized bilaterally symmetrical. Behind the motor cortex lie the sensory regions. The sensory areas receive and process information from the skin, bones, joints and muscles and the movement of the body through space. This region sometimes is called the haptic area. The bilateral symmetrical pattern of organization seems to hold true for both the motor and sensory areas of the brain. The left side of the brain controls the right hand and foot, while the right cerebral cortex controls the left side of the body. The sensory and motor areas of the brain are specialized to the degree that every area can be linked to the control of a particular part of the body (Figure 2).

The occipital area, in which vision takes place, is at the back of the head just above the brain stem. The occipital area also is symmetrical in both hemispheres. The information from the left visual field of both eyes goes to the right hemisphere and the information from the right visual field goes to the left hemisphere. Although each hemisphere receives information from both halves of the visual field, one eye will tend to be dominant, sending a greater percentage of the visual information to the dominant hemisphere. The right eye sends more information to the left hemisphere; the left eye sends more information to the right hemisphere. The dominant hemisphere is the hemisphere that appears to respond more often or appears to be dominating the response (Figure 3).

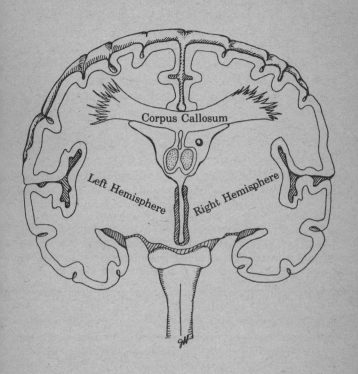

**Figure 1.** The Corpus Callosum.

The Corpus Callosum is the major nerve fiber connection between the two hemispheres.

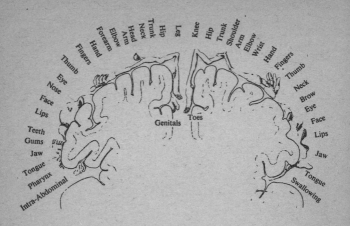

**SOMATIC SENSORY AND MOTOR REGIONS** of the cerebral cortex are specialized in the sense that every site in these regions can be associated with some part of the body. In other words, most of the body can be mapped onto the cortex, yielding two distorted homunculi. The distortions come about because the area of the cortex dedicated to a part of the body is proportional not to that part's actual size but to the precision with which it must be controlled. In man the motor and somatic sensory regions given over to the face and to the hands are greatly exaggerated. Only half of each cortical region is shown: the left somatic sensory area (which receives sensations primarily from the right side of the body) and the right motor cortex (which exercises control over movement in the left half of the body).

**Figure 2.**   Specializations of the Human Brain.
From "Specializations of the Human Brain"
by Norman Geschwind.

4

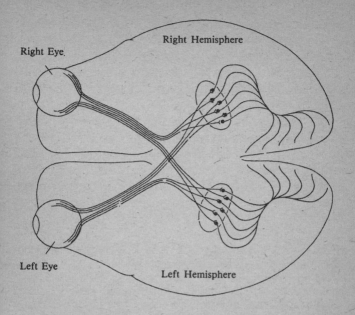

VISUAL PATHWAY is traced schematically in the human brain, seen here from below. The output from the retina is conveyed, by ganglion-cell axons bundled in the optic nerves, to the lateral geniculate nuclei; about half of the axons cross over to the opposite side of the brain, so that a representation of each half of the visual scene is projected on the geniculate of the opposite hemisphere. Neurons in the geniculates send their axons to the primary visual cortex.

**Figure 3.** Visual Pathways.
From "Brain Mechanisms of Vision"
by David H. Hubel and Torsten N. Wiesel.

Although sensory stimuli to each ear go to both sides of the brain, the input to the opposite side usually is stronger. Simply stated, information given to the right ear is sent first to the left hemisphere and then to the right hemisphere.

As noted, the brain is not totally symmetrical. Many specialized functions seem to be centered primarily in one hemisphere or the other. The speech and hearing centers are on the left side of the brain just above the ear (Broca's area). The sound memory area is behind the

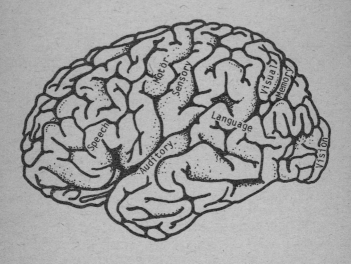

**Figure 4.** The Left Hemisphere.

A view of the left hemisphere, indicating the areas involved in specific functions.

hearing center. Although the language area, known as Wernicke's area, is in the left hemisphere for the majority of people, it can develop in either hemisphere (Figure 4).

Before we go any further with this anatomy lesson, let's have some fun with our own brains. Close your eyes and picture a chocolate ice-cream cone. Put your finger on the part of your head where you imagine you can see the cone. If you can't see it, don't worry. Try to picture something else and put your finger on your head where the picture is. If you can't picture anything, try to hear the words "chocolate ice-cream cone." Now put your finger where you imagine you hear the words. Keep your finger on your head and open your eyes.

By doing this exercise you will become aware of the visualization and auditory areas of your own brain. Hearing is usually above the left ear, visualization in the middle of the forehead or slightly to the right, and haptic or motor/sensory awareness at the top of the head.

Used in a group situation, these activities make you realize how different brain patterns are. Some people are aware of visualization in the frontal area, some slightly to the right, and others cannot localize the awareness.

People who can visualize very well usually are processing in the right hemisphere; their comprehension takes place by seeing pictures. They are called **visual learners.** Those who comprehend by hearing (**auditory learners**) usually are processing in the left hemisphere.

Those who cannot localize their comprehension usually are **haptic learners;** they learn by experience. I have found these people to be right-hemispheric or to alternate from one side to the other.

When we talk about a right- or left-hemispheric person, we are talking about learning preferences based on the functional differences between the hemispheres (hemispheric specialization).

There are different theories explaining the development of hemispheric specialization. One theory promotes the idea that up to the age of four years the brain hemispheres develop symmetrically. The functions that develop on one side of the brain also develop on the other. The two sides mirror each other. Thus, if a child suffers a brain injury before the age of four, the uninjured side of the brain has the capability to take over most of the functions of the injured side. The child usually grows up able to function normally. At the age of four years, the two hemispheres begin to specialize. Each side of the brain develops strengths in different cognitive functions. This specialization is complete by five.

At the age of five, lateral integration begins. Lateral integration is the stage when the two sides of the brain begin to interact so that the child can process something in the left visual field, send it to the right brain, transfer it over to the left brain, interpret it and deal with it on a manipulative or written level. Supporters of this theory believe that although functional specialization is complete by the time most children start kindergarten, lateralization is not complete until about the age of nine.

A second theory proposes that hemispheric lateralization, or dominance, and functional specialization are present before or at birth. The theory holds that there is a gradual activation of the specialized functions as the child is exposed to environmental stimuli. Lateralization is not apparent until the neural connection (corpus callosum) between the hemispheres has completely developed, at about the age of five or six. Specialization and lateralization are believed to be complete by the age of nine.

A third theory suggests that lateralization for language is present at birth but that specialization of other functions in the brain develop over time and are not complete until puberty.

Perhaps all of these theories are correct. The potential for hemispheric specialization of language may be present at or before birth, with other areas of specialization developing as the child experiences life and matures. Specialization may go through several developmental stages, the first being when the child begins to talk. The second stage occurs around the age of five, when he begins to understand symbolic representations and chooses a dominant hand. The last stage occurs around puberty, when specialization is complete.

Or is it?

Regardless of the theories, teachers and parents have observed many five-year-olds who are constantly changing hands while they are drawing, cutting, or just playing. Teachers know that while many kindergarten children have difficulty learning certain skills or concepts, learning comes easily for these same children by the age of nine.

Many children starting kindergarten have not developed a motor or hand dominance. Their hemispheres are still in the process of some form of specialization or lateralization. Five-year-olds and even six-year-olds are not ready to do some of the tasks demanded by today's curriculum. Children usually are not ready to handle pure abstract information until the third grade.

In general, young children are not ready for the paper-pencil symbolic and abstract type of teaching we now do. When they seem to be answering, they may well be regurgitating information and not processing it internally. These children learn by experience. They learn through concrete and manipulative methods. They need time to grow and mature.

For many years, the dominant hemisphere automatically has meant the hemisphere dominant for language, or the left hemisphere. Since new research has indicated that in some people dominance for language is in the right hemisphere, the above concept no longer is appropriate. When I talk about the dominant hemisphere, I am referring to the hemisphere activated for most tasks, the hemisphere that is the stronger of the two.

All of us use both hemispheres of the brain but we may use one side more than the other. For instance, you might have a dominant right hemisphere, which simply means that it is your preferred or stronger hemisphere. It is the one with which you tend to process first most of the information you receive. That doesn't mean you don't use your left hemisphere. You may use your right hemisphere 60 percent of the time and your left hemisphere 40 percent. Similarly, when we talk about right-brained or left-brained children, we do not mean they use only one hemisphere but simply that they use one hemisphere to a greater extent than the other.

Hopefully, the hemisphere that dominates also will be the hemisphere that is more skilled in processing the information received. This is not always what appears to happen. In some cases, a child will prefer to use the right hemisphere even when the left hemisphere may be more appropriate for the task. I have found that these very right-brained children often are failing in school.

Rigidity of specialization should not be over-emphasized. There generally is a balance between the hemispheres, with each taking control of the tasks it is best at handling.

To make this concept more practical, let's talk about hemispheric specialization as it relates to **academic skills.** Certain skills have been assigned to either the left or the right hemisphere. Although research is not complete in this area, it is clear that differences do exist. Table I lists the skills or curriculum area strengths generally attributed to left and right hemispheres.

## TABLE I.  SKILLS ASSOCIATED WITH HEMISPHERIC SPECIALIZATION

| LEFT HEMISPHERE | RIGHT HEMISPHERE |
|---|---|
| handwriting | haptic awareness |
| symbols | spatial relationships |
| language | shapes and patterns |
| reading | mathematical computation |
| phonics | color sensitivity |
| locating details and facts | singing and music |
| talking and reciting | art expression |
| following directions | creativity |
| listening | visualization |
| auditory association | feelings & emotions |

Handwriting tends to be in the left hemisphere. So is the ability to interpret symbols of any kind such as number and letter symbols. Most areas of language, including verbalization, phonics, reading, the ability to deal with details and facts, the ability to follow directions, hearing, and auditory association, are in the left hemisphere.

These are the skills children must handle on a day-to-day basis in the classroom. We give children symbols; we stress reading, language, phonics; we ask for details; we insist upon directions being followed; and, mostly, we talk **at** children. In short, our curriculum is left-brained. We teach to the student who has a dominant left hemisphere.

In the right hemisphere are a whole other set of skills. The right hemisphere has the ability to recognize and process non-verbal sounds. It also displays a greater ability to communicate using body language.

Although the motor cortex is in both hemispheres, the ability to make judgments based on the relationship of our bodies to space, needed in sports, is basically centered in the right hemisphere. The right hemisphere also seems to be involved in the interpretation of haptic information processed in the sensory regions.

The ability to recognize, draw, and deal with shapes and patterns as well as geometric fugures—circles, squares, triangles, rectangles—lies in the right hemisphere. This involves the ability to distinguish between different colors and hues, as well as the ability to visualize in color.

Singing and music are in the right hemisphere. Creative art is in the right hemisphere. While many left-hemispheric children are quite good in art, the "art" they make is structured; it must come out a certain way. Their pictures, or the things they create, are the drawings they make for Mother's Day or the turkeys they draw for Thanksgiving. Left-hemispheric children are very good at directed art.

Right-hemispheric children I have observed create "mystery" pictures. They show the pictures to you but you aren't quite sure what you are looking at until you are told. They might show raindrops falling and the sun shining at the same time. Perhaps they will draw bullets being fired from a boat. Many right-hemispheric children will draw cartoon bubbles containing words from a story that exists only in their heads.

When you ask these children what they have read, they can retell the story in their own words without any difficulty. However, they are so creative that they usually add their own details and ending. You think they are exaggerating and, yes, they are exaggerating in our terms. But in their terms, they are simply being what they are. They change stories, add details, and alter endings to meet their emotional needs because feelings and emotions appear to be in the right hemisphere.

Each hemisphere of the brain also specializes in a different **mode of consciousness.** Two separate and unique ways of processing stimuli exist within each person. Although both hemispheres receive and process sensory information from the surrounding environment, each hemisphere processes the information separately.

In short, the right brain and the left brain have specialized thinking characteristics. They do not approach life in the same way, yet both hemispheres use high-level cognitive modes.

The left hemisphere approach to life is part-to-whole. It sequences and is logical. The right hemisphere learns whole-to-part. It does not sequence; it looks at things holistically, in an over-all picture.

Table II contrasts left and right modes of consciousness.

## TABLE II.   MODES OF CONSCIOUSNESS

| LEFT HEMISPHERE | RIGHT HEMISPHERE |
|---|---|
| linear | holistic |
| symbolic | concrete |
| sequential | random |
| logical | intuitive |
| verbal | nonverbal |
| reality-based | fantasy-oriented |
| temporal | non-temporal |
| abstract | analogic |

**Linear and Holistic.** Linear means part-to-whole. The left-brained person takes little pieces, lines them up, arranges them in logical order, and arrives at a convergent conclusion. The right-brained person thinks whole-to-part, holistically. The child with a dominant right hemisphere starts with the answer, a total concept, or perceives the whole pattern and discovers a divergent conclusion. Very often he experiences difficulty with sequential thought.

Today, most reading instruction is aimed at the left hemisphere. It is logical and sequential. Phonics is built on part-to-whole, on sequence. Learning the sounds is done part-to-whole, in sequence.

But what happens to the children who have to learn whole-to-part? What happens to the child in school who cannot learn phonics, who can learn only the whole word? He stays in phonics until the third grade—and he still cannot read! He's started on his career of failure in school.

**Symbolic and Concrete.** Left-hemispheric children think in symbols; they deal with symbols; they can function with symbols. Right-hemispheric children deal with the concrete; they learn by doing, touching, moving, being in the middle of things. If they can't hold something or feel it or pick it up, it really doesn't exist for them. They often need this concrete experience before they can visualize.

Right-hemispheric children must deal with real money; they don't want to play with paper money. They often have difficulty dealing with dittos or any other written activity sheet. This is an important consideration as you begin to realize that one or more of your children may have a dominant right brain.

**Sequential and Random.** The left brain approaches life sequentially, while the right brain floats randomly through life's experiences. My husband and I have a lot of fun with this. I'm married to the most left-brained, sequential lawyer in the whole world. Everyday he knows exactly what he's going to do. How does he know? He makes a list, numbers it, and goes sequentially through the list, crossing off tasks as he completes them. I, on the other hand, make no lists and muddle through the day's tasks quite at random. Some things never get accomplished and sometimes six additional chores are rapidly dispatched. My husband doesn't understand how I get anything done.

This is a good time for you to take stock of yourselves. If you do **not** think sequentially, well, the Lord bless you, for you will need His help. Do you think sequentially? Good. Please add us non-sequential thinkers to your list, under the category of "people to pray for."

The world thinks everything is sequential. But many people simply do not think that way. Certainly many children do not think that way, **and they never will.** They think randomly and if you try to force them to think sequentially you will cause a lot of ulcers, create a lot of headaches, and waste a lot of time. I leave it up to you to decide whose ulcers, whose headaches, and whose wasted time.

**Logical and Intuitive.** Logical, that's my husband. He knows exactly where he gets his answers. He starts out with a little piece of information and logically works toward an end result. Right-brained children are intuitive; they are not logical. They pull the answers right out of the air. They can give you the answer to a long-division problem but they may not be able to work through the sequential steps. They can look at fractions, can know that ¼ is less than ½, but cannot explain why. The sad thing is that these children honestly do not know why they can't explain why something is so. They want to know; they want to be like their classmates; it hurts them not to know.

We often accuse these children of cheating because they give an answer but cannot tell where, how, or why they got it. Not so. They function intuitively. This is the way they think. Often they come up with answers more quickly when left alone than when made to conform to the rules.

**Verbal and Nonverbal.** Left-hemispheric children are very verbal, usually possessing good vocabularies. They have no difficulty expressing themselves. Right-hemispheric children are considered non-verbal; that is, they have difficulty expressing themselves. They can use an object, they can touch it, they can point to it if you

18

ask them to identify it, but they may experience problems labeling it.

**Reality-based and Fantasy-oriented.** Left-hemispheric children can deal with reality, with the way things are. They can deal with the pictures and stories they are given in school. Left-hemispheric children are very much affected by the environment and will adjust to it. If something is presented to them, **they** will shift and react. That is the way they go through life. If something is not there for left-hemispheric children, it doesn't exist for them.

Right-hemispheric children will try to change the environment, to make **it** shift and react to meet their needs in any way they know how. This tendency often shows up as behavior problems in these children. They deal with fantasy, with imagery, with imagination. They are more comfortable creating from within.

I remember Kevin, who was always late for school. One morning, with big brown eyes turned upward, he announced, "I met this unicorn that wanted directions to the nearest rainbow, and he promised me you wouldn't be mad." That was the last straw. "Kevin," I yelled, "you know unicorns aren't real!" With a look of complete indignation he yelled back, "Unicorns are real!"

During the year I learned that, to Kevin, unicorns were very real.

**Temporal and Non-temporal.** This is one of the hardest areas to deal with. Left-hemispheric children have a sense of time. Right-hemispheric children have very little sense of time. They simply do not comprehend when you set time limits. "In ten minutes" might as well be "in a few days." "Before lunch" might mean "before lunch next Thursday." They cannot think in any terms except the here and now. This minute, right now—this is it for right-hemispheric children. They cannot judge time; they cannot complete their work on time; and, frequently, they cannot get to school on time. That is way timed tests are so difficult for them. When they are taking a test, they either will be finished way ahead or will still be in the middle of the test when the bell rings.

**Abstract and Analogic.** Left-hemispheric children can deal with abstract explanations as we present them. We simply have to tell these children that "this is the way it is." They can accept that very easily. Right-hemispheric children learn through absurdities, the more absurd the better. This applies especially in the area of discipline.

I will never forget the day I met a little six-year-old monster. Everyone had tried everything—all without success. No one could get him to behave. I approached him, purse in hand. I held up the purse, making sure I had his undivided attention, and asked, "Do you see this purse?" "Yeah," he replied. "Do you know what I keep in there?" "No." "Well, I'll tell you. It's full of little boys' heads that I unscrew when they won't behave."

Absurd? Yes, of course. But it worked. He never gave me any more trouble. Right-hemispheric children really can transfer absurdities right into their systems. They have no difficulty dealing with them.

Just make sure that your absurdities are so way out that they can't possibly be true. And have fun!

"There is no such thing as
'best' in a world of
individuals."
—Hugh Prather

# 2
# Modality and Dominance Screening

Most children are not totally left-brained or totally right-brained. There are children who have a dominant right hemisphere with their language in the left hemisphere. There are children who have a dominant left hemisphere with language in the right hemisphere. Some children are extremely right-brained; some are extremely left-brained. Others vary in the degree of dominance of either hemisphere. Brain patterns are as individual as fingerprints. There are many combinations of dominance, all of which are normal.

Although this book talks mainly about right-hemispheric children, or those children whose hemispheric organization makes it difficult for them to learn in today's educational system, remember that many children cope very well regardless of their hemispheric organization.

As educators and parents, we need to be able to identify when a child's preference for right-brained or left-brained thinking patterns is preventing the realization of his highest potential. I have found three screening methods helpful in determining a child's dominant hemisphere; observation, a dominance screening checklist, and open-ended questioning.

# OBSERVATION

For those who do not want to bother with systematic screening and would rather make a determination from observing the child at home or at school, the following is a list of behavioral characteristics displayed by many right-hemispheric children.

1. Appears to daydream.
2. Talks in phrases or leaves words out when talking.
3. Uses his fingers to count.
4. Draws pictures on the corners of his homework papers or dittos.
5. Has difficulty following directions.
6. Makes faces or uses other forms of nonverbal communication.
7. Displays fine motor problems (cutting, writing, or pasting) when asked to conform or do structured tasks. Fine motor problems rarely appear when the child is doing something he has selected.
8. Is able to recall places and events but has difficulty in recalling symbolic representations such as names, letters, and numbers.
9. May have difficulty in phonics or decoding skills.

10. Is on the move most of the time.
11. Likes to work part-way out of his seat or standing up.
12. May exaggerate when retelling an event in which he has been involved.
13. Often has a messy desk.
14. Has difficulty in completing his work on time.
15. Likes to take things apart and put them back together again.
16. Displays impulsive behavior.
17. Tries to change the world to meet his own needs.
18. Likes to touch, trip, and poke when relating to other children.
19. Goes to the pencil sharpener often.
20. Gets lost coming to the classroom.
21. May forget what he went to his room to do.
22. May be very good in athletics but poor in subjects such as English.
23. Will give the right answer to a question but will be unable to tell you where it came from.
24. Will often give responses that are unrelated to what is being discussed.
25. May be a leader in the class.
26. May chew his tongue while working.

Not all right-hemispheric children will display all of the above characteristics and children who are laterally balanced will display both left- and right-hemispheric characteristics. Temper any decision that you make about hemispheric dominance with the fact that there still is much to learn about the human brain.

# DOMINANCE SCREENING CHECKLIST

How can we really know whether a child has a dominant right or left hemisphere? Actually, there is no real way of knowing, but, by combining the various methods of educators, neurologists, and psychologists, we can come closer than ever before. The following screening methods were chosen by looking at many different methods of determining hemispheric dominance in children and selecting those that appeared the most reliable. By combining a number of approaches, we were able to achieve a more holistic picture of a child's dominance. The items should be given as a whole, not in pieces. Remember that when dealing with the human brain there are no absolutes. The purpose of the screening is to give you an idea of a child's hemispheric preference for learning so that you can more accurately develop strategies for teaching that child or for helping him deal with his environment.

# TABLE III. INDICATORS OF HEMISPHERIC DOMINANCE

## A SCREENING CHECKLIST

Eye Dominance
Hand Dominance
Hand Position
Muscle Testing
Body Symmetry
Eye Movements

# EYE DOMINANCE

The dominant eye is the stronger eye. It usually is opposite the dominant hemisphere. That is, if the child demonstrates a dominant left eye, it indicates a dominant right hemisphere. If he demonstrates a dominant right eye, it indicates a dominant left hemisphere.

The child may use one eye when tested with his eyes open and the other when tested with his eyes closed. In this case, the eye preference with the eyes closed indicates the hemispheric dominance, while the eye preference with the eyes open may indicate the motor dominance.

DIRECTIONS:
1. Use any round tube the child can look through (plastic or paper). Stand directly in front of the child.
2. Hold the tube with both hands. If you hold it with only one hand, the young child will tend to reach out to the nearest hand.
3. Have the child stand with his feet directly under his shoulders. If the feet are aligned with the shoulders, the body is in complete balance and you will get more accurate results.
4. Say to the child, "I want you to reach out

and take this tube with one hand and look through it with one eye."

5. Say to the child, "Now, close your eyes, reach out, and put the tube to the eye that is more comfortable."

It is important that you test the child with his eyes open and with his eyes closed. Do not administer these one after another; the child usually will use the same hand if you do not provide time between the two tests.

# HAND DOMINANCE

As stated previously, the right brain controls the left side of the body and the left brain controls the right side of the body. Knowing this, we can observe which hand the child uses more often and conclude which hemisphere is dominant. Left-handers are almost always right-brained. Right-handers may be either right- or left-brained. Many natural left-handers have become right-handed from pressure of adults or the right-handed environment.

When asking the child to do the following tasks, note the hand he uses for each one. If he changes hands from one task to another or starts a task and switches hands, he is demonstrating one of the following:

   a. lack of dominance—a sign of immaturity;
   b. mixed dominance—indicates a cross-dominant pattern (dominant right eye, dominant left hand);
   c. ambidexterity—indicates the ability to use both hemispheres equally well; or
   d. alternating dominance—indicates the child is alternating hemispheres (jumps back and forth without control).

DIRECTIONS:
1. Ask the child to write his name, draw a shape, or copy a math problem.

2. Have the child throw a ball or bean bag.
3. Observe the child eating or ask him which hand he uses when he eats.
4. Have the child close his eyes and pick up several objects that have been placed in front of him.

# HAND POSITION

Since a right-handed child may be either left- or right-brained, we need a way to look at the right-handed child that is more discriminatory. Recent research has indicated that the position in which a child holds his pencil when writing may indicate a hemispheric preference. If a right-handed child holds his pencil in a straight position with the wrist straight and the pencil aimed toward the shoulder, the left hemisphere is probably dominant. If a right-hander rotates his hand or aims the pencil at a right angle to his body, he is probably right-hemispheric.

DIRECTIONS:
1. Place a paper and pencil at the child's midline (the center of his body).
2. Ask the child to write his name.
3. Compare his hand position to those in the drawings following.

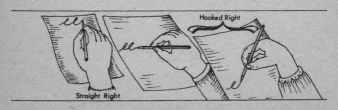

# MUSCLE TESTING

Muscle testing is a way of measuring the relative strength of the muscles as they relate to hemispheric dominance rather than muscular development. Test both sides of the body and compare their strength. The stronger side usually is opposite the dominant hemisphere.

If both sides are strong, the child may be using both hemispheres selectively in relation to the task.

If you are unable to determine a stronger side or if both sides are weak, have the child do the cross-lateral march (p. 56) and retest. If you are unable to determine a dominance, he may have mixed dominance or be alternating from one hemisphere to the other.

DIRECTIONS:
1. Place the child directly in front of you with his head straight.
2. Put his feet about 4 inches apart or directly beneath his shoulders so that his body is balanced.
3. Have him close his eyes.
4. Position one arm at a 90-degree angle from his body, or extend straight out from the shoulder.
5. Put two fingers on the wrist of the extended

arm, placing your other hand on the opposite shoulder.

6. Explain to the child, "I'm going to try to push your arm down. Don't let me."

7. Look for a locking of the muscle or a definite demonstration of strength.

# EYE MOVEMENTS

A number of research studies have indicated a relationship between habitual eye movements and hemispheric dominance. When one hemisphere is stimulated or activated, the eyes turn toward the opposite side of the body. This is another example of the control of one side of the body by the opposite hemisphere. Thus, if the left hemisphere is working, the eyes will turn right. If the right hemisphere is working, the eyes will turn left. Under stress, the eye movements appear more reliable. Stress usually causes the child to activate the dominant hemisphere rather than the appropriate one.

DIRECTIONS:
1. Stand face-to-face with the child, making sure that you have eye contact.
2. Ask the child a series of questions requiring both verbal and spatial answers.

3. Watch the child's eyes to see which way they turn when you first ask the questions.
   a. What did you have for dinner last night?
   b. What does happy mean?
   c. Where is your bed in your room?
   d. How do you spell your name?
   e. What is the answer to two plus three? (Use a problem appropriate to the child's level.)

Observation of eye movements can be used to identify the child's primary learning modality. Since the auditory center is in the left hemisphere, movement of the eyes to the right suggests an auditory learner. Eye movements to the left suggest the child is a visual learner and right-brained.

Some children move their eyes up toward the top of their head rather than right or left. These children seem to be haptic learners and often have no real hemispheric preference. Haptic learners learn through body movement and tactile information. They learn through experience.

# BODY SYMMETRY

Most of us have noticed that one side of our body is slightly larger than the other. When buying shoes, we learn quickly which foot is larger. If you wear glasses, you know which ear is higher. The side of the body that is the larger, higher or fuller usually is **opposite** the dominant hemisphere.

DIRECTIONS:
1. Ask the child to remove his shoes and socks. Place his heels against a wall. Note which foot is the longer.
2. Look at the child's ears to discover which is the larger and higher.
3. Ask the child to smile. Watch to see which side of the mouth goes the higher.
4. Hold a piece of paper down the middle of the child's face so that you can see both sides. One side will be fuller; one eye may be higher and one side will appear happier.

If your observations appear confusing, the child may have a mixed motor dominance— that is, a dominant right hand but a dominant left foot. When this occurs, processing motor information and accurately accomplishing motor tasks can be confusing and difficult for the child.

41

# OPEN-ENDED QUESTIONING

Piaget and others have always believed that we could learn the most about children by observing, listening to, and talking with them. Moshe Feldenkrais, in his book *The Case of Nora,* explores the importance of asking questions to discover what is happening in the brain. In doing your own questioning, let your intuition lead you to your next question. Remember, every child's cognitive organization is as unique as his fingerprints. Stereotyped techniques or questions will not work. It also is important to relate the questions to the task the child is having difficulty accomplishing.

The following are examples of open-ended questions and my interpretations of the child's responses. These responses indicate both hemispheric dominance and learning modality (visual, auditory, or haptic).

A **visual** modality usually indicates right brain dominance; **auditory,** left brain dominance; **haptic,** generally a right brain dominance or a child who is alternating between the two hemispheres.

1.  **Question:** I want you to see your favorite ice-cream cone in your head. Where do you see it? (Be sure the child is familiar

with the object you ask him to visualize.)
**Interpretation:** If the child points between the eyes or a little to the right, I have found it indicates he is a visual learner. If he points to the top of his head or puts his whole hand on his head, he probably is a haptic learner. Both of these responses indicate a right-hemispheric learning style. If he cannot visualize, ask him the following questions requiring auditory activation.

2. **Question:** Listen inside your head. I want you to hear your favorite song, birds singing, or waves hitting the beach. Where do you hear the sounds?
**Interpretation:** If the child points to the left side of his head, my experience has indicated that he is an auditory learner and probably left-brained. If he points to the same area as he did when asked to visualize the ice-cream cone, it reinforces your conclusion that he is a visual learner. Some children are both visual and auditory learners and will respond to both questions appropriately. This also suggests that they are able to selectively use the hemispheres.

3. **Question:** What did you have for dinner last night?
**Interpretation:** This question requires the child to combine visualization and memory. Watch the eye movements and ask him where he remembers it. Some children will

43

say they cannot remember. If this occurs, ask the child to visualize his environment.

4. **Question:** Close your eyes. See the table. See yourself sitting at the table. Take your fork and put some food on it. Bring the food to your mouth. What is on the fork?

   **Interpretation:** If the child can remember only when asked to involve his own body in the memory process, it indicates he is a haptic learner. He learns by doing and remembers by recalling what he did. These children often feel that they cannot remember. Our job is to teach them their individual style of remembering.

5. **Question:** Here is a new word. The word is _____. I want you to learn it. (Give the child sufficient time.) How did you learn it?

   **Interpretation:** If the child is able to learn the word easily, you can record his method of learning and help him recognize the process. If the child appears to learn the word immediately but cannot recall it later, the word may not be going into the long-term memory or the child may not be able to retrieve the word. Examine the child's responses to Questions 3 and 4. Is the child incorporating the modality he uses to remember actual experiences into learning symbolic representations such as numbers, letters, and words?

6. **Question:** Can you see a circle in your head? (Ask the child if he can visualize his

environment, shapes, colors, pictures, numbers, letters, or words.)

**Interpretation:** The extent of his ability to visualize will tell you if he has internalized the cognitive concepts. It also will indicate which teaching materials to use when presenting a new concept.

I became aware of how important it is to use the right materials while working on addition with seven-year-old Johnny. I went into his classroom and showed the teacher how he could do addition by visualizing cracking eggs into a skillet. Johnny did beautifully. Two weeks later, the teacher came to me and complained that when I left, Johnny stopped adding. The teacher was using square counting blocks to teach addition. When I asked Johnny to visualize the shapes, we discovered that he could not visualize a square but could visualize a circle. As long as the teacher used round manipulative objects, Johnny could add. Our next job was to help Johnny internalize the square.

7. **Question:** (Ask the child to see the number four in his head.) Draw what you see. Now see four things in your head. What do you see? Draw what you see.

**Interpretation:** These questions give you information as to how the child has internalized number concepts. Does he see dots, lines, or environmental objects? Does he see them vertically, horizontally, or in patterns? This information will help you to know how to present number concepts, whether to use such materials as dice, or whether vertical or horizontal flashcards would be more effective.

8. **Question:** (Show the child a word he already knows.) What is the word? How do you know? How do you remember it?

    **Interpretation:** This question not only makes the child aware that he has a way of remembering but also gives you information about his style of retrieving information. If he retrieves it auditorily, then he needs to say it inside his head during the learning process. Some children are visual learners but retrieve information through the auditory or haptic system.

9. **Question:** What can you remember about your classroom? Tell me everything you remember.

    **Interpretation:** The child's answer to this question will give you information about the types of sensory information he is attending to and clues about his preferred learning modality. Note whether he is giving auditory or visual descriptions.

10. **Question:** How do you remember what your mother/teacher wants you to do?

    **Interpretation:** This question tells you how the child processes auditory information within his environment. Some children will tell you that they can't remember. These children are having difficulty processing auditory information and may need visual input to remember.

# HEMISPHERIC DOMINANCE SCREENING

| TEST | RIGHT DOMINANCE | LEFT DOMINANCE |
|---|---|---|
| 1. Eye Dominance | | |
|     Open | L | R |
|     Closed | L | R |
| 2. Hand Dominance | L | R |
| 3. Hand Position | Hooked | Straight |
| 4. Muscle Testing | L Stronger | R Stronger |
| 5. Body Symmetry | L Larger or Higher | R Larger or Higher |
| 6. Eye Movements | L - Visual Haptic | R - Auditory |

7. Open-ended questioning

NOTES:

## SCREENING: Sample, Boy—8 Years Old

1. Eye Dominance
   eyes open - right eye
   eyes shut - right eye
2. Hand Dominance - right hand
3. Hand Position - straight
4. Muscle Testing - right arm stronger but left arm showed strength.
5. Body Symmetry - sides seem equally full.
6. Eye Movements - eyes turn right and left.
7. Open-Ended Questions - processed information visually and auditorily.

INTERPRETATION:

The child has a dominant left hemisphere, but uses the right hemisphere almost as often. He learns by seeing and hearing. Because of his age, he will still need to experience many things for optimal learning.

"All I want is for you to accept me as I am."
—Hugh Prather

# 3
# Learning Strategies

Each child's brain is unique. When we look at learning methods to help children, we need to remember that each child has his own learning style which is right for him. Our job as parents and teachers is to support our children's individual learning styles by providing a holistic environment both at home and school. Several basic premises underlie the holistic approach to learning.

First, each child is the center of his own universe. He sees the world as it relates to his inner understanding, not yours. Learning takes place within this universe. It doesn't take place on a ditto, on a walking beam, or while doing homework. Learning takes place in the child's brain and that brain is inside the child.

Second, we tend to forget that the child can learn only to the maximum of his own experience. If a child is from a family where he is not talked to, that child is going to have difficulty in language because he has not experienced it. Children learn by connecting new information to past experiences. The richer and more varied their environmental experiences, the more apt children are to learn with ease.

Third, children's learning styles appear to be affected by their dominant hemisphere. Children should be exposed to both left-hemispheric and right-hemispheric areas of curriculum as well as the left and right modes of consciousness. If either hemisphere is totally ignored, it becomes less and less able to function.

Fourth, there are different sensory modalities through which a child learns. A child may be selectively able to learn visually, auditorily, and haptically or he may learn more effectively through just one of the modalities. When working with a child, first teach to the child's strongest modality and reinforce the material through the other modalities.

Fifth, a child's learning ability is affected by nutrition, biochemistry, and ethnic cultural experiences.

Finally, be sure the approach you are using is working. Regardless of what the screening or other test results have indicated, regardless of what methods have been suggested, if the approach is not working, "dump" it. Children have the right to enjoy learning, whether they are working at home with their parents or in the classroom.

The learning strategies presented are all right-brained in their approach...that is, they use one of the characteristics or skills attributed to the right brain to introduce the concept. This does not indicate that I do not believe in left-hemispheric approaches. It does indicate that I believe there already are enough left-hemispheric approaches in today's curriculum.

# CROSS LATERAL MARCH

When the screening list indicated that a child had one hemisphere that overshadowed the other, especially when the dominant hemisphere was the right one, a short-circuiting or blocking seemed to occur. Having these children move their bodies in a cross-lateral pattern seemed to balance the two hemispheres and alleviate this blockage.

Have the child stand in a balanced position with feet directly under each shoulder. Move his body in a cross-lateral pattern...that is, the right arm should move simultaneously with the left leg and the left arm with the right leg. When he understands this movement, have

him do ten on each side. If he has difficulty standing and moving, allow him to lie on the floor and do the same movements or to touch each knee with the hand on the opposite side of his body.

At first the balancing effects of these movements will be only temporary. However, you must repeat them several times a day, especially when the child appears unbalanced or is handling a difficult activity. With repetition, the period of balance extends itself. It seems to have a cumulative effect.

To test the effectiveness of the cross lateral march, have the child read part of a story before the activity and another part after. Be sure he does not read the same part each time. If the reading is smoother and more expressive and the child appears more relaxed after the exercise, it will be beneficial to use it with him over an extended period of time.

The first time I tried using the cross lateral march, I was very doubtful. My first guinea pig was a fourth-grade boy named John. He was a very poor oral reader. His teacher asked him to read. His reading was jerky and he missed several easy words. We asked him to do the cross lateral march ten times. John read again; the words seemed to flow out of his mouth. I don't know who was most shocked—John, his teacher, or I.

It is not necessary to take time from teaching to include cross lateral march activities. The children can march on the way to the reading group or they can march back from lunch or to music.

At home, the child can march to his room, while watching television, or while exercising.

# HAPTIC ACTIVITIES

The haptic system is the system of information that comes from our skin, the movement of our joints, and the movement of our bodies through space. It is the tactile and kinesthetic modes combined. Haptic differs from gross motor movement in that it often involves the visualization of the environment or symbol involved in order to accomplish the task. It may involve the sensory motor area of the cortex.

Although the haptic system is activated whenever there is body movement, it functions at a higher level when we block out visual sensory input by closing our eyes. All of the following exercises should be done with the children's eyes open, then repeated several times with their eyes shut.

a. writing in the air;
b. tracing numbers, letters, or words;
c. moving the body to form a shape, number, or letter;
d. writing on the child's back;
e. walking a number, letter, or word; and
f. associating a body movement with a symbol or group of symbols.

# SENSING THROUGH TOUCH

In many children, senses conflict or are confusing. Encourage children to use all their senses, but one at a time. Start with vision. Give each child an object or piece of fruit. Explain that everything has shape, size, color, and texture and takes up space. Have each child explore his own object until he visually understands it. Next, have the children close their eyes. Explain that by touching, you can discover some of the same information as you can with your eyes open. Now have each child rub the object and listen to the sound, bounce it, hit it on the table or desk, etc.

When the children have understood the concept, present a word and have them explore it with each of their senses.

1. What can you discover by just looking at the word (e.g., size, number of letters, configuration, small words, familiar sounds)?
2. Trace the word. What does it feel like?
3. Close your eyes and visualize the thing the word names. What does it look like? What does it feel like? Does it have any uses?
4. Hear the word inside your head. What does it sound like? Does the thing it names make any sound?

# WHOLE-WORD APPROACH

Many children who tested right-brained on the checklist had difficulty with any type of phonics. Single sounds were disastrous for these children. Here is what usually happened. I would ask the children to sound out the word "mop." They would say, "Mmm-ooo-p." I would respond, "Beautiful—what is the word?" They usually responded with something like: "Cat"! They could not take pieces and put them together. I had to give them a whole word to learn.

The following procedure worked well:

1. Write the word on the chalkboard or a chart.
2. Write each letter a different color (this is called color-shock).
3. Have the children say and spell the word with their eyes open, then with their eyes closed.
4. Have the children close their eyes and visualize the word.
5. Have the children hear the word inside their heads without moving their lips.
6. Have the children write the word three to five times with their eyes closed.

# PHONICS

Phonics requires the ability to discriminate and associate sounds to make a word. These skills are basically located in the left hemisphere and are a part-to-whole activity. To change the process to a whole-to-part activity, start by teaching the children several sight words containing the same pattern such as "fat," "cat," and "sat." Ask the children how the words are alike. It is important that the children discover this by themselves. Once they have discriminated the visual likeness of the words, ask them to think of new words that have the same ending. Explain that we call this rhyming. Write the words they think of on the chalkboard. Now you can begin to show the children some words you have thought of. Do

this by adding letters to words already on the chalkboard or by changing letters. Do not write new words without connecting them in some way to the words the children already know. The activity is more effective if the children write the words themselves and make the substitutions by erasing a letter or letters and replacing them with ones they think of themselves. A small chalkboard that they can hold is helpful.

# SEQUENCING EVENTS

Although the right-hemispheric or right-brained children seemed to do beautifully in telling fantasy stories or retelling events that they themselves had experienced, they did not do well in sequencing a series of events within a paragraph or sequencing a story they had previously read. To help these children with this concept, I involved their whole body and thinking process in the activity.

Begin by giving the children a paragraph with a sequence of events that is very obvious; have them read the paragraph, and discuss it with them. Then have them cut the paragraph into sentences and mix them up. Finally, have them paste the sentences back into the paragraph that they started with. For a more difficult task, give the child a short story and have him read it, cut it into paragraphs, scramble it, and paste the paragraphs into the correct order. Both of these tasks will help the child understand the concept of sequencing.

Vary the task as follows:

1. Give the children three or more sentences. Have them find the sentences in a paragraph or story and underline them in different colors. Next, using the matching color,

have them number the original sentences in the order they happened.

2. Give the children a number of sentences. Have them find the sentences that are the most like them in a paragraph and paste them on top of these sentences.

3. Give each child a different paragraph or short story. Have the children design sequencing activities for each other. Have the child who designed a particular activity check to see if it was done properly.

# SEQUENCING USING BODY MOVEMENT

I found that some children learned the concept of sequencing more quickly by going through a series of body movements. Show the children a series of body movements. (Hands on head, touch the shoulders, and bend over.) Ask the children to show you what you did first, second, and third. Show them another series of movements. Ask them to tell you what you did second, first, and third. Repeat and ask them to draw what you did. Ask them to read three or four sentences, then have them read a short story and tell you which sentence was first, second, etc. Finally, have them label the sentences as to their sequence.

This last method came to me intuitively when I was working with a group of second-grade children who just didn't seem to be able to grasp the concept of sequencing. We looked pretty silly doing the activity but after fifteen minutes the children could sequence the sentences in a story.

# STORY PROBLEMS

Right-brained children have difficulty handling more than one concept at a time. These children are unable to do story problems because they require dealing with number concepts and word concepts simultaneously.

The following are various methods that can be used to approach the problem. Have the children draw pictures of what is happening in the story problem, using the exact number of desks, chairs, and so forth, and counting them to get the answers. Have the children read only the words leaving out the numbers, and tell you what is happening. Have the children act out the story problem. Show the children the key words that will help them decide whether to add, subtract, multiply, or divide. Once the children begin to be able to visualize what is happening in story problems, you will find they have little or no difficulty working them.

# EXAMPLES:

**A.** Jack had 3 bags of candy. Each bag had 7 pieces of candy in it. How many pieces of candy did Jack have?

$$3 \times 7 = 21$$

**B.** The train left Center City at 11 o'clock A.M. It took two hours to get to Dover City. What time did it get to Dover City?

# TEACHING SYLLABLES

The concept that words can be divided into parts is difficult for the child who sees the word as a whole unit.

Using body movement to emphasize the concept may help. Say a compound two-syllable word and ask the children to say it with you. Tell the children to imagine two body movements to go with the word. It is important that they find their own movements. Do this with several words until the children can discover the two movements with ease. Explain that they have just divided the words into syllables. Write the words on the board, showing the divisions by color-coding each part. Have the

diff    er    ent

children divide other syllabolic words by visualizing the body movements. As the children become proficient, proceed to more difficult words and body movements.

# OPPOSITES

Understanding the concept of opposites should take place before you ask children to memorize paired opposites. By using opposite words that involve emotional feelings or changes in awareness, you can involve the whole body in teaching the concept of opposites.

Ask the children to close their eyes and relax. Tell them to pretend their whole body is the word "cold." Suggest they visualize the word in a cold color, picture something cold, feel their bodies getting colder, become chunks of ice that form the letters of the word "cold," and move their bodies the way they would if they were cold.

Have the children relax and be themselves. Tell them that hot is the opposite of cold. Have them experience being hot (e.g., visualize, picture, feel, move). Discuss the differences in feelings. Use such words as happy-sad, like-dislike.

As the children feel the changes in their bodies and emotions, they will internalize the differences in the meanings of the two words. This technique can be used to teach any vocabulary concept.

# THE CLOCK BODY

Since right-brained children appear to have little or no concept of time and its organization, it often is very difficult to teach them time as it appears in the academic situation. It also is difficult to teach them to read a clock. By combining visualizations, body image, physical movement, and bringing the entire environment to the child, time becomes a very personal concept for the child.

Have the children close their eyes and pretend they are clocks. Have them extend their arms above their heads and move them around in a circle as they have seen the hands of a clock move. Have them put their arms in different positions and tell you what time they think they are saying. You may be surprised to discover that they already know the different times but cannot express them.

If you find that a child has no concept of time, start by having him put both arms directly above his head in the position of 12 o'clock. It is most helpful for many children to have a visual model of a real clock that has been taken apart so that you can reach the hands and move them manually. If you use your own body as the model, be sure you face the same direction the children are facing.

Then do the one o'clock position, the two o'clock, and so forth.

Once you have taught the hours, you need to evaluate the children you are working with to discover whether it would be easier to teach the half-hours and quarter-hours first or the minutes. Whichever you decide to teach first, have the children use their arms to demonstrate the positions of the clock hands. To make it less awkward for the children, you may want them to switch their arms when they reach the half-hour. It is important that the child be able to do this with his eyes open, following a model, and also be able to indicate a specific time with his eyes closed.

Once the child can demonstrate the various times with his body movement, he then needs to learn to transfer the concept onto paper. Many children are unable to transfer information directly from the gross motor activity to paper. These children need a fine motor activity between the two steps in order for information to transfer. Have the children make clock faces out of paper plates, using pegboard, cardboard, or popsicle sticks for the hands of the clocks. Be sure one hand is shorter than the other. For children who learn easily by listening, call out the various times and have the children put the clock hands in the right position. For children who are visual learners, write the time on the board and have them place the clock hands in the correct position. When the child has completed this task, he should be able to make the transfer onto paper, drawing the hands in their proper positions on clock faces that appear on dittos.

# TEACHING THE HOUR

The more children involve their own bodies in learning, the more quickly understanding and ownership of a concept take place.

Draw a large circle on the chalkboard, approximately four feet in diameter. Write the numbers 1 through 12 on the circle to form a clock face. Tell the children to pretend they are clocks. They can be any kind of clock they want (i.e., grandfather, alarm, etc.). Pictures of different clocks will help them visualize.

Have the children stand and place both hands at the 12 o'clock position.

1. Have them imagine that the arm that stays on the 12 is longer than the other arm.
2. As you call each hour, have the children move their right arm to the number position. When they get to 6 o'clock, have them switch arms.
3. When the children can find the correct position with their eyes open, have them do the same movements with their eyes closed. (Repeat several times.)
4. Say the hours at random. Have the children find the appropriate body positions.
5. Give the children a ditto page of clocks. Each time you say an hour, have them visu-

alize their body position and draw the arms on the clock faces. Remind them which arm is longer.

6. Write the hours on the chalkboard (e.g., one o'clock, three o'clock) in random order. Have the children point to the correct time as you say the words.

7. Give the students dittos with the words at the top and complete clock faces at the bottom. Have the children use a green crayon to underline the time word you say. Say the word again. Have the children use the same color to underline the matching clock. Change color for each time. Finally, have the children paste the correct time words under the matching clock face.

8. Reinforce by asking individual children the time throughout the day, visualizing the various times or using clear, simple dittos.

# TEACHING THE
# HALF-HOURS

Many children find it easy to learn to tell time by the hour but experience difficulty when presented with the half-hour. Follow the procedures for the hour, with the following variations:

1. Draw a clock face on the chalkboard, making one half green and the other half yellow.
2. Have the children put both their arms at the 12 o'clock position. Draw the arms on the clock face. Show that the longer arm begins to move around the clock. This means time is passing. Explain that when the long arm gets to the number 6, the hour is half over. We call this six-thirty.
3. Have the children move from 12 o'clock to twelve-thirty several times with their eyes open and closed.
4. When you are sure they have the concept, you may present the other half-hours. **Always** start with the hour and move to the half-hour.
5. Use the same concept to teach the quarter-hours and minutes.

# GROUNDING

Focusing the child's attention on a reading page is called grounding. Grounding to the reading pages before reading silently or orally allows children to skim the pages, focus visually on words, and become familiar with material on the pages before they read. Grounding can be done by:

1. Discussing the picture:

    a. What's happening?
    b. What time of day is it?
    c. What will happen next?
    d. How do you feel?
    e. What colors do you see?
    f. How many children do you see?

2. Asking the children to quickly find:

    a. A specific word.
    b. A period.
    c. A question mark.
    d. The first word on the page.
    e. The last word on the page.

3. Asking the children to *quickly* point to a word that:

    a. Begins with the sound of _____.

b. Ends with the sound of _____.
c. Means _____.
d. Means the opposite of _____.
e. Is the name of a girl, boy, animal, etc.
f. Is a color word.
g. Tells what time of day it is.
h. Tells how the _____ feel.

4. Asking the children to read orally.

# SIMPLE ADDITION

When teaching beginning addition, use manipulatives or semi-concrete representations (paper punch dots, rice, or macaroni). Have the child paste the counters beside the numbers.

EXAMPLE:

$$\begin{array}{r} 2 \ \bullet\bullet \\ + \ 3 \ \bullet\bullet\bullet \\ \hline \end{array}$$

Some children need to see a whole pattern. Have these children place the counters where the answer will go:

EXAMPLE:

$$\begin{array}{r} 2 \\ + \ 3 \\ \hline \bullet\bullet/\bullet\bullet\bullet \end{array}$$

I discovered this concept while working with five first-grade children who just didn't seem to be learning to add. I used counters, paper punch dots, sandpaper letters, etc. Nothing worked until I began to present the answers as whole patterns. Suddenly the lights went on. When they could see the answer as a whole, they understood.

# COLUMN ADDITION

There are many different ways to approach column addition. Most texts teach adding from top to bottom. This method seemed very difficult for some of the right-hemispheric thinkers.

I helped these children look for patterns within the problem. Some patterns that appeared helpful were: pulling out 10's; grouping numbers (i.e., all the 6's or 5's); multiplying numbers (i.e., starting with the largest number); or mixing the processes.

Ask the children to find other ways to solve the problem.

$$
\begin{array}{r}
4 \\
2 \\
6 \\
5 \\
1 \\
+\ 3 \\
\hline
\end{array}
$$

a. has eight "2's" and a "5" or
$16 + 5 = 21$

b. has two "10's" and a "1" or
$20 + 1 = 21$

c. $\quad 4 + 2 = 6$
$\qquad 6 = 6$
$\quad 5 + 1 = \underline{6}$
$$
\begin{array}{r}
18 \\
+\ 3 \\
\hline
21
\end{array}
$$

# CARRYING

The right-hemispheric child often has difficulty with the concept of "carrying" because the most common method of teaching carrying separates the number by placing half of it at the bottom of the page and the other half at the top.

EXAMPLE:

$$
\begin{array}{r}
{}^{1}42 \\
\times 6 \\
\hline
2
\end{array}
\quad \text{or} \quad
\begin{array}{r}
{}^{1}49 \\
+15 \\
\hline
4
\end{array}
$$

This can confuse the child who sees the number as a whole. Often he will reverse the numbers, carrying the wrong one.

To eliminate this confusion, have the child carry the number at the bottom:

EXAMPLE:

$$
\begin{array}{r}
49 \\
+\ 15 \\
\hline
{}^{1}4
\end{array}
$$

Another method of doing this kind of problem actually eliminates the need to carry. Have the child add left to right, adding the tens or hundreds first and working backwards.

EXAMPLE:

$$
\begin{array}{r}
49 \\
+56 \\
\hline
90 \text{ - tens} \\
+\ 15 \text{ - ones} \\
\hline
105
\end{array}
\qquad \text{or} \qquad
\begin{array}{r}
394 \\
+783 \\
\hline
1{,}000 \text{ - hundreds} \\
170 \text{ - tens} \\
7 \text{ - ones} \\
\hline
1{,}177
\end{array}
$$

$$
\text{or} \quad
\begin{array}{rrcrcr}
394 = & 300 & + & 90 & + & 4 \\
+\ 783 = & 700 & + & 80 & + & 3 \\
\hline
& 1{,}000 & + & 170 & + & 7
\end{array}
$$

# SUBTRACTION

There are many different ways to teach subtraction using the "whole" concept. The following are a few:

1. When teaching borrowing to those who can't grasp the concept, try having the child add the same number to both subtrahends so that the bottom subtrahend ends with a zero.

EXAMPLE:

$$84 + 2 = 86 \qquad\qquad 643 + 22 = 665$$
$$- \qquad\qquad\qquad \text{or} \qquad -$$
$$68 + 2 = \underline{70} \qquad\qquad 278 + 22 = \underline{300}$$

2. The following method was used many years ago and may be helpful to some children. Add a ten to the top number on the right and a ten to the bottom number on the left, then subtract.

EXAMPLE:

$$84 = 80 + 14 \quad \text{one ten is added to the four to}$$
make fourteen

$$-$$

$$\underline{68} = \underline{70 + \phantom{0}8} \quad \text{one ten is added to the 6 to}$$
make it 70

84

3. Have the child subtract by adding. Start with the small number; using your fingers or counters, count until you reach the large number. The number you counted is your answer.

EXAMPLE:

$$
\begin{array}{r}
9 \\
-7 \\
\hline
2
\end{array}
\quad
\begin{array}{cc}
\text{(say)} & \text{(count)} \\
\text{seven} & \text{eight, nine} \\
& \bullet \quad \bullet
\end{array}
$$

# NINES TABLES

When presenting the nines multiplication tables, use a whole-to-part haptic approach. Write a multiplication fact on the chalkboard, e.g., 3 × 9. Have the children hold both hands up. Tell them to count 3 fingers and fold the third finger down. They will have 2 fingers, a space, then seven more fingers, or an answer of twenty-seven. This works only with the nines tables. Do the same with 4 × 9, 5 × 9, 2 × 9 and so on. Practice by showing the children a fact by using your hands and having them write the problem.

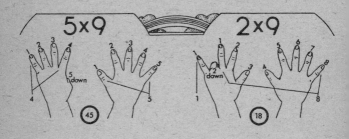

# PUZZLES

I was working with some children at a school last year who could not put any puzzles together and were being labeled as having severe eye-hand coordination motor problems. I watched these kids and they were movers. They were up and down, in and out, and they'd rather draw pictures along the side of the dittos than anything else. They were having a great time. They just couldn't put puzzles together. So I took the puzzle and put it together for one child. Then I had him take one piece at a time, move it to one side, and put it back in place again. He had no trouble. Next I dumped the puzzle onto the desk and he put it together beautifully. Why? Because I had shown him what it looked like when it was all put together. When children are having difficulty putting a toy or project together, have them work whole-to-part. This is done by:

1. Having the child see the completed product.
2. Having the child take it apart step by step.
3. Having the child visualize the end results while he is working.
4. Giving the child a visual model.

# ORGANIZING FEELINGS

Right hemispheric children may become very frustrated with their lack of academic success. Their emotional response and behavior may become inappropriate. The following will help the children gain control of and learn to express their feelings.

1. Several times during the day ask the children to tell you how they are feeling about what they are doing.
   EXAMPLE: "How are you feeling?" "How is it changing your body?" "Are your feelings keeping you from completing your work?"
2. Have the children lie on the floor with their eyes closed. Ask them questions about how they feel physically.
   EXAMPLE: "How do your arms feel?" "If you move them, do you feel better?" "Does any part of your body hurt?" "Can you do anything to make yourself feel better?" "If you relax, does it stop hurting?"
3. Have the children use different tones of voices and talk about how they feel.
   EXAMPLE: "For the next half hour, everyone has to shout when they talk." "Now, I want you to use a soft, caring voice." "See if

it makes you feel differently." "Do others treat you differently?"

4. Give the children old magazines and have them cut out words and pictures that tell something about how they feel and what they like or dislike. Have the children paste them on paper to make a "me collage." Then guess which collage belongs to which child.

5. Have the children write their names in large letters on plain paper according to how they feel.

EXAMPLE: "Make the letters the shape you feel about yourself: tall, thin and so forth."

"Pick a color that feels like your name and trace the letters."

"Draw pictures around your name that tell how you feel about yourself."

# HOME AND SCHOOL ORGANIZATION

Cleaning their desks and organizing their bedrooms are not talents the right-hemispheric children generally display. By using their natural attraction to color and size, parents and teachers had success in teaching them how to organize in the class room and at home.

1. Use different colored folders for keeping the homework papers for each subject. Be consistent for the whole class or grade level.
2. Paint sections of the closet rod in different colors. Organize the closet by color or shape. Put all the blue clothes together or hang the pants on the red color and the shirts on the blue, etc.
3. Have the child organize his desk by size (put the largest or thickest book on the bottom, etc.). You also may use colored book jackets to help the child remember which book is which.
4. Make the children responsible for room organization. At home or at school, use color, shape, size, and visual pictures to show where objects are to be put.
5. Have the child number his dittos in different colors in the order you want them com-

pleted. That is, the ditto with the green number one is to be done first, the ditto with the blue two second, etc. The child must write the colored numbers on himself or he will not remember which color comes when.

6. To help at home:
   a. Color-code the silverware drawer.
   b. Trace the silverware on place mats.
   c. Put colored drawer handles on the dresser to designate the sock drawer, underwear drawer, etc.
   d. Organize the child's own closet.

Sometimes the activities help the parents as much as the child. One parent wrote, "When I first heard your methods, they sounded so simple that I couldn't believe them. I had to take them home and try them. Having my son clean his room by picking up all the blue things first, the red things next, etc. was amazing. It still doesn't stay clean for very long but it does get cleaned when I ask."

# VERTICAL WRITING

The children who tested right-hemispheric had a natural tendency to function directionally from their dominant hemisphere toward their non-dominant hemisphere, or from right to left. This would be no problem if they were learning Chinese, but since our language has a left-to-right orientation it seemed a definite problem. These children transposed words in sentences, mirror wrote, reversed letters like "b" and "d," and reversed the order of letters within words.

Vertical writing organizes the letters of a word so that the right-hemispheric child can deal with them comfortably.

h         diff

e         er

l         ent

p

Write the vocabulary words on the chalk-board, sequencing from top to bottom (see example). Have the children say each letter of the word and name the word. When you have repeated this several times, have the students write the words vertically and horizontally on their papers.

# WORKING AT RANDOM

When given a large number of math problems, some children tire before they reach the end of the task. Others become discouraged when they come to a problem they can't do. The problems at the beginning of the task will be done but will not necessarily be correct and the children may never get to the ones at the end. Instead of having them start from the top of the page and work to the bottom, have them select the problems they want to do. This allows them the freedom to do the problems they understand. This will raise their self-image and they will do twice as many problems.

This approach works with any type of independent activity.

At home, make a list of the chores you want the child to do and let him choose the order in which he wants to complete them. Remember, children and adults of any age take more pride in anything they have had a part in planning or arranging.

# ORGANIZING PROCESSES

When faced with a mixture of math processes on one page (e.g., addition, subtraction, and multiplication), many children become confused. Susan could do addition, subtraction, and multiplication problems when there was only one problem or only one kind of problem on the page. The minute she had to do a mixture of problems, she became confused and could not complete the work.

To eliminate the confusion:

1. Try to present only one kind of problem to a page.
2. Show the children how they can do all the addition problems first and then do all the subtraction problems.
3. Have the children identify the different kinds of problems by coloring the addition signs green and the subtraction signs red, etc.
4. Have the children copy all the multiplication problems in green, the addition in blue, and the subtraction in red.

# TEST TAKING

If you analyze the way you take a test, you may find that you have developed a procedure that enables you to complete the test in the most efficient way. Right-hemispheric children seemed to do better at test taking if they were taught to do the following:

1. Scan the whole test; do the part that is the easiest.
2. Work through the test, reading each question or math problem. Do only those you are sure you know. Put a check by those you think you know and a question mark by those you think you don't know.
3. Working from the front or the back of the test, do all the ones you think you know. Try several methods of remembering:
   a. Visualize the answer.
   b. Picture yourself looking for the answer in the book.
   c. See the teacher standing in front of the class giving the answer.
   d. Close your eyes and write the answer that comes to mind.
4. Go back to the questions you don't know. Use the memory methods listed above. If none of these work, do the following:

a. Eliminate the answers you know are wrong.
b. While relaxing, take three deep breaths and write or circle the answer you feel is right.

# ORGANIZING MATH PROBLEMS

Although the right-hemispheric children usually had an excellent understanding of spatial relationships in their environment, if often was difficult for them to organize or align numbers and letters on a page. Many of them received poor grades because the teachers could not read or follow their work. Others made errors in their work because the numbers were not in the proper place value location. David was one of these children. No matter how hard he tried, his problems usually came out looking something like (A) below.

To help children like David, turn their notebook or writing paper so that the lines go up and down (B). There is now a column for the ones, tens, and hundreds. Use this for multiplication, division, or large addition problems.

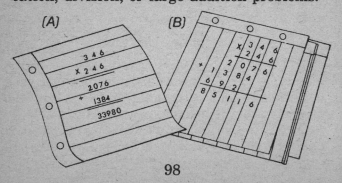

# COLOR GROUNDING

I found that the children who tested right-brained on the screening instrument seemed very sensitive to color. They could tell me how color tasted, how it made them feel, and which colors they associated with which people. Understanding this, I could better relate to the fact that these children reacted to the different colors I wore, to a colored classroom, or to the color their bedroom was painted, or related better to toys of a specific color.

When the children were helped to understand their own relationship to colors and how specific colors were affecting them emotionally, they began to have some control over their own behavior. I had an assortment of colors available so that the children could select the color that made them feel calmer, made them feel good, kept their attention longer, or helped them work better. They covered their work area with this color, placing their ditto or homework on top of it so that they were surrounded with feelings of that specific color. Since children are very changeable creatures, it did not work to use the same color everyday. Children needed to be able to select the color that met their needs on any one day.

Often the children demonstrated positive changes in behavior and concentration. One child in particular never seemed to stop moving. He seemed everywhere at once, always at the wrong time. His favorite color was red. When I asked him why the color red made him sit still and think better, he said, "It makes me feel warm and heavy. The others make me want to fly."

I still am not sure why color grounding seems to work, but the important thing is that, in many cases, it does work.

At home, allowing your child to select a color that he is most comfortable with for his own bedroom, play area, or clothes often removes stress and allows him to feel more centered.

# COLOR WRITING

As previously stated, the children who tested right-brained had a special affinity for color. They often reacted emotionally to colors and were visually attracted to bright colors.

Using this concept, have the children write their spelling words, vocabulary, or multiplication tables in color-shock. This is done by writing each letter a different color. Make the first letter green, indicating go, so that the child knows where to start. The other letters may be any color.

Color writing seemed to help many of the children who had difficulties in directionality, visual discrimination, and sequential memory.

Green  Orange  Blue  Red  Black

# COLOR

Lisa had been reversing the letters of her name for two years. After writing her name in color on everything she did for one week, the reversals disappeared.

Jimmy was failing all of his spelling tests.

He began to practice his spelling words in color. Now he passes all of his tests and even gets some 100's.

**COLOR WRITING!**

# RAINBOW LETTERS

Children love rainbows. They love the colors and the fantasy of a rainbow. Use this association to give them the same feeling about letters.

Read a story about rainbows, look at pictures of rainbows, and, if possible, see a real rainbow.

Give each child a model of the letter or letters he is having difficulty with. Have him use crayons to trace around the letter with each color to make a rainbow of letters.

Add the following variations:

1. Make a rainbow wall. By making each child's name in a different color, you can make a large rainbow on the wall.
2. Paste the rainbow letters in the sky of a picture.
3. String the rainbow letters across the ceiling.
4. Make a rainbow scrapbook. Put a rainbow letter on each page and paste pictures from magazines around it in the shape of a rainbow.
5. Color each letter a single color so that you have a "B" for each color in the rainbow. When all the letters are done, arrange them in a rainbow.
6. Make a cursive rainbow.

7. Make rainbow writing paper. Have the children color each space a color of the rainbow.

# TEACHING DIRECTIONALITY

Most children understand that a green traffic light means go and a red traffic light means stop. By placing a green mark or dot on the left side of a writing paper and a red one on the right, the child can be taught to start at the left and progress to the right.

The following are a few of the creative ways this concept can be used:

1. Color the beginning letter of a sentence green and the punctuation mark red.
2. Color the beginning of each paragraph green.
3. Put a green dot on the left hand and a red one on the right hand.
4. Put green and red dots on the desk, door, dittos, etc.
5. Color the top line on the writing paper green and the bottom line red. (Use different colors for children who are red/green color-blind.)

# DYED RICE

Ordinary rice can easily be colored by soaking it in food coloring overnight and allowing it to dry out.

Give children examples of written conversation, addresses, contractions, abbreviations, etc. Be sure the commas, periods, and quotation marks are correctly placed in each example.

Have the children paste or glue blue rice on the quotation marks, red on the commas, or green on the apostrophes. After the children have done this successfully for two or three days, have them complete an activity where they must paste the rice in the proper place without a visual model.

The children also may glue red rice under all the verbs, blue under the nouns, etc.

Whenever you combine color with an eye-hand coordination activity, you increase the sensory stimulation even further.

# WORD PATTERNS

Color can be used to emphasize the sameness of words. Children can easily identify patterns in words when the patterns are color-matched.

On the chalkboard or on flip cards, write several words containing the same pattern (e.g., light, fight, sight). Write the pattern (ight) in the same color in all of the words. Write each of the other letters in a different color. Explain to the children that if the color stays the same, the sound stays the same; if the color changes, the sound changes.

This same concept can be used for math problems such as: $2 + 3 =$, $3 + 2 =$, or $1 + 4 =$. The problems that are written in the same color have the same answer.

It is important to have the children do their own writing in color to reinforce the concept.

# BORROWING

When learning subtraction, some children do well until they are asked to regroup or borrow. It seems that no matter how many times you say, "Take the bottom number from the top number" they will subtract the smaller number from the larger:

EXAMPLE:

$$\begin{array}{r} 34 \\ -27 \\ \hline 13 \end{array}$$

Color-code numbers, making the top number red and the bottom number green. Say, "Take the green number from the red number." By using color to organize their thinking, the children seem able to grasp the concept.

EXAMPLE:

$$\begin{array}{r} 34 \quad \text{(red)} \\ -27 \quad \text{(green)} \\ \hline \end{array}$$

For older children who are dealing with more complex problems, have them color or circle the numbers they must change.

EXAMPLE:

$$3\ 4\textcircled{0}8\textcircled{2}$$
$$-\ 1\ 2\ 6\ 4\ 3$$

# ONES - TENS - HUNDREDS

Again, use color. Write the words "ones," "tens," "hundreds," "thousands," and "millions," each in a different color. Hang them in the classroom where the children can easily see them. Explain to the children that if they write numbers in the color in which you have written the word "hundreds," they will be called hundreds. Write several examples of numbers on the chalkboard, e.g., 212, 429, 634, in the corresponding colors. Have the students read the numbers as a group. Then call on individual children to read specific numbers. For several days, have the children copy numbers from the chalkboard, using crayons or magic markers to write them in color on their papers.

# 214,103,027

| green | red | blue |
| for | for | for |
| millions | thousands | hundreds |

# VISUAL MODELS

As I have mentioned many times, right-brained children often are visual learners. They may need to see a picture of the completed task before they can visualize what they are to do. Teachers and parents may provide this support in the following ways:

1. When asking the child to complete a structured craft activity, provide a completed sample for him.
2. When asking the child to practice the mastery of a new concept, do an example for him.
3. Do the first problem on a math paper or reading ditto.
4. Place charts in the room to remind the child how to head their papers.
5. If you use color-coding a lot, be consistent and provide a visual clue. For example, if the children are using yellow folders to keep their math papers in, then provide a yellow container when they turn in their work.

# CONFIGURATION

Some children need more than a sight word approach to reading. They need added stimuli to reinforce the "whole word" concept.

Write a word on the chalkboard and trace around it with colored chalk, giving it a configuration.

EXAMPLE:

Have the children visualize the word and its shape. Do this with several words. On one side of the chalkboard, draw the configurations and on the other side, write the words. Have the children match them. Give the children configurations. Have them write the correct word in each. Have the children copy the words and give each a configuration. Have the children make puzzles out of each configuration.

Use the following variations:

1. Outline with yarn, rice, etc.
2. Make configuration flash cards with the word written on the back.

3. Cut colored paper in the shape of words.
4. Say a word and have the children draw the configuration.
5. Give the children several configurations of words. Have them write a sentence using only the configuration. Have fun by:
   a. Having them read their sentences.
   b. Having them guess each other's sentences.

# OBSTACLE WORDS

Some words are difficult for children to learn because they have no concrete representation. Have the children write a word on newsprint. Have them visualize the word as an obstacle course. Which letters can they jump over, climb, crawl, or slide down? To reinforce the concept, have the children tell a story or draw pictures of what they would do with each letter. Explain that they must do something with each letter. It is helpful to do the first word together.

EXAMPLE:

h e r e

1. jump through the         h
2. hang from the             e
3. slide down the            r
4. hang from the             e

# CREATIVE DITTOS

Dittos can be boring. Be creative. Ask the children to think of all the different things they could do with a ditto without using a pencil. To get them thinking, suggest the following:

1. Glue pieces of yarn or rice under the answers.
2. Instead of coloring the pictures, make mosaics of rice or paper.
3. Glue yarn over the plus and minus signs to remember the processes.
4. Cut the ditto apart and reorganize on writing paper.
5. Use environmental material, e.g., real grass, twigs, or leaves, to add to the picture.
6. Make puzzles out of the dittos.
7. Cut magazine pictures and add to the pictures on the ditto.
8. Have the children design their own dittos. Choose some for the whole class to do.

# CHALKBOARD

There are children who learn beautifully standing up. But sit these children down and they forget it all. For example, one fifth-grade girl could take her spelling tests at the chalkboard and get 100%. Sitting down to take them, she failed every time. From that point on, we had her learn all of her spelling words and take all of her spelling tests at the chalkboard.

Right-hemispheric children seem to be movers. They sit halfway out of their seats; they sit with one foot tucked under their behinds. They have to go to the bathroom more often than anyone else in the class. And they sharpen their pencils until they are nothing but stubs. They learn while they are moving and many of them MUST be standing up or moving in order to learn.

The moral of all this, of course, it to get your children out of their seats and up at the chalkboard. I can recall my own school years. We went to the chalkboard and we stayed there until we learned our arithmetic. Some days, I stayed at the board all day, but I did learn arithmetic. And other children in their seats learned through watching my efforts.

I urge you to try this in your own classroom the next time you teach an arithmetic lesson.

Put your so-called right-hemispheric children at the chalkboard doing problems while your left-hemispheric children are in their seats working the same problems on paper. You will find that you are teaching both groups at the same time.

Parents can easily do the same thing at home.

# LAP BOARDS

If you are the type of parent or teacher who can't tolerate the seeming confusion caused by standing children, have them use lap boards.

Lap boards are small chalkboards used by children at their seats. Using them requires a shoulder movement, thus involving the gross motor muscles.

Put an arithmetic problem on the chalkboard and then have the children do the problem on their lap boards. By instructing the children to hold up their boards when they have finished the problem, you will quickly be able to determine which children understand the mathematical concepts involved. Mnay different concepts can be taught or reinforced in this way. Anything that can be written on paper can be written on a lap board.

For example, your children can use their lap boards to:

1. Take a trial spelling test.
2. Practice manuscript or cursive letters.
3. Write creative thoughts while listening to music.
4. Practice number facts or spelling words.
5. Divide words into syllables.
6. Practice answering test questions during review.

# CRAWLING LETTERS

Some children are functioning on a very low level of gross motor development. To reach their stabilized learning level, these children need to crawl.

When teaching such children their numbers or letters, use masking tape to form letters three to five feet in diameter on the floor. Have the children crawl the letters using a cross-lateral crawl, the right arm moving with the left leg. It is important that they repeat the name or number of the letter as they crawl its shape.

One teenager on his school's swimming team could not learn his letters at all in the traditional manner. We had him swim his letters and he learned them all in one session. He went on to learn individual words and finally was able to read. When asked how he learned new words, he looked very surprised and answered, "Why, I just swim them in my head."

# TOOTHPICK ME

Toothpicks, popsicle sticks, or other similar materials are very effective in teaching body image. By allowing the child to represent his own body by building toothpick people, you enable him to see the relationship between his body parts and how they are connected.

The trunk and chest parts of the body may be formed by building a square out of four toothpicks. The child may break the toothpicks into small sections to form the neck. Each arm is formed from two toothpicks so that the child can see that it bends at the elbow. The legs are formed in the same way, with a small separate piece for the foot so that the child can see that the foot bends away from the leg. Since we do not want the children to get the idea that they are squareheaded, it is advisable to give the child a small round piece of paper to form the head.

If the child cannot place the toothpicks in the right positions without a visual model, you may provide magazine pictures and have him place the toothpicks over the various parts of the body. We have found that if the visual models are toothpick people, the child does not make the association with the real body.

Toothpicks also can be used in teaching the

child letters of the alphabet. Many of the letters, such as "A" and "H," are made up of sticks, while others are made up of circles. With toothpicks and circles, the child can put all of the letters together.

# INTUITIVE READING

I have worked with many special children, but the highlight of my teaching experiences came when I worked with a fourth-grade boy who could not read. It was obvious that Michael was intelligent. He just couldn't read.

Although I felt no real hope of helping Michael, two hours later he was reading on a third-grade level with complete comprehension. We were both surprised. I was even more surprised when he went on to finish the fourth-grade book within a few weeks' time.

I need to explain here that Michael did not learn to read in two hours. It is my belief that he had been taking information having to do with reading and vocabulary and storing it in the right hemisphere. Yet he had been trying to read and decode out of the left hemisphere. When I showed him how to center his thoughts on the right hemisphere and pull the words out intuitively instead of trying to decode them, he was able to retrieve the information that had been stored all of these years.

Hoping this was not a once-in-a-lifetime experience, I set out to try the method on other children. To my utter surprise, and delight, it worked. Many children were able to jump to their appropriate grade level and maintain the skills.

1. Ask the child to read for you so that you get an idea of his normal performance. Be sure to use reading material he has been taught.
2. Say to the child, "See your favorite color in your head. Put your finger on your head so I know where you are seeing it." (This lets you know they are really seeing it and reinforces the color for them.)
3. Say to the child, "Keep the color in your head. When you open your eyes, I want you to read but don't think about the words, think about the color in your head. If you don't know a word, let your color tell you what it is." Have the child open his eyes and read.
4. The reading should be fluent.
    a) If the child begins to sound a word or stops at a word, have him close his eyes, visualize the color and look for the word in the color.
    b) If the fluency diminishes and the child begins to read word by word, stop him and start with the color again.
    c) You will need to repeat the procedures many times until the child automatically closes his eyes and retrieves the word or words by using the color.

Although the method does not work for all children who are poor readers, it works for some. It seems to work the best on children who are in the third grade or above.

124

# JUMPING JACKS

Learning spelling words can be fun if it is done outside on the playground or with the P.E. teacher.

First, be sure the children you are working with can do a jumping jack. If they can't, you may use hopping, jumping, toe-touching, clapping, or any one of several body movements.

So that the children can see them with ease, write the spelling words on large flash cards, the larger the better. Hold each card up in front of the children and instruct them to say and spell the word **before** they do any moving. Then have them do as many jumping jacks as required to spell the word letter by letter. The word "help" will require six jumping jack movements, as follows:

help

h

e

l

p

help

You will be amazed at how quickly your children learn to spell!

# TEACHING COLOR

When we talk about the concept of whole-to-part, we have to include the child's whole environment. Children learn first in their total environment and we need to take a close look at the information the child already has learned before we begin to teach any new concept.

A good example of this is the teacher who said to me, "I have a little girl who isn't learning her colors and I have done everything." I suggested to this teacher that she take the child outside and find out what colors the child did know. When she asked the child what color the grass was, the child said, "Green." When she asked what color the sky was, she answered, "Blue." Yet the child could not identify a green or a blue crayon. When the teacher took the crayons outside to the child's environment and showed the child that the green crayon was the same color as the grass, the child immediately make the connection between the information that she already knew and the symbolic information that the teacher was trying to teach.

The teacher also unknowingly had included another whole-to-part concept in her teaching methods. By presenting the child with several colors of her environment at one time, she was giving the child a holistic picture of color and allowing her to observe the differences between them. Presenting one color at a time would not have given the child a holistic picture.

# ROLLING IN COLOR

Right-hemispheric children enjoy learning through experience and tend to learn more quickly when they can experience the thing they are trying to learn. Rolling in color allows children to totally experience the color and attach an internal meaning to it.

To enable children to roll in color, use cloth or large sheets of colored or painted paper. Have the children lie on the color face down; tell them to close their eyes and visualize the color. Then have them roll in the color and imagine it surrounding them. Keep telling them what color it is and ask them to repeat the name. Ask them to smell the color, to taste it.

Explain that colors make us feel emotions. Have them tell how they feel as they are rolling in the color.

When they have finished rolling in color, ask them to paint a picture using the color to express what they experienced.

# EATING COLOR

Any additional sensory level the parent or teacher can activate strengthens the learning process. Taste and smell are two primary sensory systems.

By using gelatin of different colors and flavors, you can provide the multisensory experience of seeing, smelling, and tasting color. Using several different packages of color gelatin, have the children open each package and smell it. Have them distinguish the differences in smells. Have them close their eyes and visualize each color as they smell it.

Allow the children to choose the flavor each one wishes to make. When the gelatin is set, have them use plastic spoons to taste it. Urge them to feel the gelatin as it slides down their throats. Urge them to imagine their bodies becoming the color of the gelatin.

If the gelatin is fruit flavored, have some of the real fruit on hand. Have the children imagine they are the fruit.

Throughout the ativity, it is important that you and your children repeat the name of the color after each experience.

# FLASHLIGHT TRACKING

When I first started teaching, I found it very difficult to get some children's attention. In desperation I used a flashlight to shine where I wanted their eyes to be looking. For me the flashlight became a very effective teaching tool.

Use the flashlight to write shapes, numbers, letters, or words on the ceiling or chalkboard. Have the children track the light with their eyes and the pointing finger of their writing hand while they are repeating the number, word, or letter.

The children will be forced to visualize the symbol you are drawing and will activate the haptic system with the arm movement.

To teach number concepts, flash the light on the chalkboard and have the children say or write the numeral that matches the number of flashes they saw. Use two sets of flashes and have the children add them.

To reinforce their spelling words, write the words with the flashlight on the chalkboard and have the children tell you the word.

Use the flashlight to speed up the children's reading. Write a story on the chalkboard or a chart and move the light along the line at the speed you want the children to learn.

This method can be used to pace reading, to teach phrasing, or to reinforce left-to-right progression.

# MAGAZINE TRACKING

Once children have learned to focus on individual words while reading, it often is difficult for them to progress to reading across a line smoothly.

Magazine tracking not only will correct word-by-word reading but also will help eliminate problems with directionality, reversals, omissions, and fixations.

Tear a page from a magazine, the larger the print the better. Ads are a good place to start. Have the children loop each vowel in each word. Be sure they do not lift their pencils except at the end of each line. Limit the activity to no more then ten minutes.

This activity may be used to reinforce any concept. Try the following activities:

1. Loop the alphabet in order.
2. Loop punctuation marks.
3. Loop "b's" or "d's."
4. Loop nouns, verbs, or adjectives.
5. Loop word families.
6. Loop all the words you know.
7. Loop the letters in your name.
8. Loop the first letter of each word.

# WHOLE-LETTER WRITING

Many right-brained children have poor handwriting skills. These children have difficulty dealing with the individual parts of a letter, remembering the shape of each letter, and naming the letter once they have written it.

One little boy put it better than I ever could when he said, "By the time I remember how to draw a circle, I have forgotten where the line goes and I don't know what I'm writing anyway!"

Whole-letter writing is an alternative way of writing letters in which the child forms the whole letter without lifting his pencil from the page. Although there is no set way of forming each letter, the preferred direction is top to bottom. The following are examples of the letters that seem to give children the most problem.

a b d e g h k m n p r u w y

# CURSIVE WRITING

For many children, transferring from manuscript to cursive writing is very difficult. These children can learn to write the letters individually but are unable to make the transfer so that they can read what they have written or are unable to look at the printed word and transfer it into the cursive.

David was very poor in English and writing. Before he could spell a word, he had to stop and think how to make each letter. By the time he had finished the word, he had lost the thought he was trying to write. By learning the cursive alphabet as a whole, Michael made the transfer from manuscript to cursive writing automatically and was able to read what he had written.

Have the children practice writing the entire alphabet three or four times a day.

EXAMPLE:

You can immediately pick out which letters are difficult for the children. Have them practice these separately. Once the children have learned to write the entire lower-case alphabet in cursive, you can then begin to teach the capitals. Since

they have made the transfer from manuscript to cursive already, these should
not be difficult for them to learn.

*abcdefghijklmnopqrstuvwxyz*

# AIR WRITING

Air writing is very much like flashlight tracking in that it provides a visual model.

Write a word on the chalkboard and have the children say it aloud. Have them close their eyes and visualize the word. Then spell the word. As you spell it, have them write it in the air, keeping their eyes shut all the while. With their eyes still closed, have them spell the word as they write it in the air. Next, ask them to see and say the word inside their heads as they write it in the air. Finally, tell them to open their eyes and write the word on paper.

Air writing may be used to teach letters, words, numbers, or anything else you wish.

# TACTILE WRITING

Tactile writing requires that children have sensory stimuli to the ends of their fingers. Any heavily textured material may be used.

Write a spelling word on plain paper and place the paper under a piece of screening. Have each child trace the word with the pointing finger of the dominant hand. The exercise should be done first with the eyes open and then with the eyes closed.

Cut letters, numbers, or words out of varying grades of sandpaper, ranging from extra-fine to coarse. Have each child again finger-trace with the pointing finger of the dominant hand. Be sure each child has the opportunity to work with each grade of sandpaper.

Use glue and glitter to make raised models of numbers, letters, or words for each child to finger-trace.

Make letters, numbers, or words out of colored pipe cleaners or use yarn, rice, seeds, macaroni, etc. to create textured models for the children to finger-trace.

Bake sprinkled cookies in the shapes of letters or numbers. Have the children hold the textured letters or numbers behind their backs and identify them by touch only. Several cookies may be aligned to form a word. Have children finger-trace the textured cookies.

Children also may be given a small tray or box of sand in which to copy letters, words, or numbers from a visual model.

Use a language master or tape recorder to provide auditory input for the children.

# FINGER PAINTING

Whenever we involve more than one stimulus that right-brained children seem to respond to, we make learning easier for the child. By using color and tactile input in the same activity, we double the odds of the child's learning.

Teachers have found that having first-grade children finger paint their reading words is one of the most effective ways for them to learn. This method may be used with any concept you are trying to teach.

The following variations take courage, but may be more fun:

1. Paint in chocolate (or vanilla or butterscotch) pudding.
2. Paint in cake frosting of various colors and flavors.
3. Paint in shaving cream or toothpaste (the new striped toothpastes are particularly colorful).

Whipped cream, yogurt, mayonnaise, mustard, apple butter, ketchup—all of these lend themselves to a somewhat messy but very valuable learning experience.

# WATER PAINTING

If you absolutely cannot live with the mess involved in creative finger painting, don't do it. Simply paint with water.

Give the child a paint brush and a small container of water. Small plastic cheese containers are excellent for this purpose. Baby food jars work well but they are breakable. Some children will need 2- or 3-inch brushes while others will do very well with half-inch bristle brushes.

Have the children practice whatever you are teaching by writing it on the chalkboard with the brush dipped in water.

If you are courageous (or perhaps crazy), give the children water pistols and let them "shoot" their words on the chalkboard.

Both of these water activities stimulate visualization, memory, and gross motor skills.

# TOOTH BRUSHING

Never throw anything away! You will be amazed to discover how many discards can be transformed into effective teaching tools. Save old thread spools, wooden clothespins, coffee cans, and especially toothbrushes. Collect all the old or new toothbrushes you possibly can. You are going to use them to stimulate the skin.

There are places on the body where there are a large number of nerve cells close to the skin's surface. These are: the cheek, the back of the hand, the bottom of the feet, and the middle of the back between the shoulder blades. You can use three of these places to stimulate the haptic system.

Using a toothbrush, write letters such as "b" or "d" on the child's back and ask him to show you, tell you, or write what he felt. This is especially helpful in correcting the "b-d" reversals.

Have a child write letters on the back of his own hand, saying the letters as he writes them.

Connect symbols and sounds by writing a letter or letters on a child's cheek. Ask the child to make the sound as you write it.

Have the child make the shape of a number with his tongue as you write the number on his hand, back, or cheek.

Make two marks on the child's back and have him hand you the number or the same number of objects.

Have one child write spelling words on the back of a second child. Have the second child spell the words.

Using an imaginary crayon, have one child make a picture on the back of a second child. Have the second child use real crayons to draw what he felt.

# WORDS AND SHAPES

By using shapes as the base of a teaching strategy, you not only utilize the right hemisphere's natural tendency for spatial relationships but you also connect a new concept to a stabilized understanding.

Write different letters on shapes made from colored paper. Press letters may be used if you prefer. Present new vocabulary by building the words from the shapes.

EXAMPLE: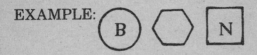

Have the children visualize the shapes and letters as they spell the word. Repeat this several times. Scramble the shapes and call on a child to find the word: BEN. By gluing felt or sticky tape on the backs of the shapes, this can be done on a flannel board or chalkboard.

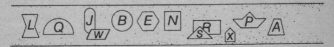

# NUMBERS AND SHAPES

Children who are extremely right-hemispheric may have difficulty counting objects and relating them to a symbolic numeral.

Use shapes to represent specific numbers, i.e.:

O = 0   ∧ = 1   ⊓ = 2   △ = 3   □ = 4
☆ = 5   △△ = 6   △□ = 7   □□ = 8
□☆ = 9   ☆☆ = 10

Have the children count the corners on the shapes. Then have them visualize the shape or group of shapes that represent a numeral. Once they have memorized the shape-symbol relationship, they may begin simple addition using the shapes.


EXAMPLE:

$$\begin{array}{r} 2 \sqcap \\ + 3 \wedge \\ \hline \end{array}$$


Have the children make up their own number system. When I asked one second-grade class to do this, I got some interesting examples such as: daisies, dice, clocks, pennies, and random objects.

I then introduced Roman numerals. The children who had been counting on their fingers did the problem using the Roman numerals.

EXAMPLE:

$$II + V = VII \text{ or } 7$$

# SOUNDS AND SHAPES

Children sometimes are caught in situations where they must learn phonics. In such a situation, we again need to fall back and look at the concept areas that the children can handle. If they are very good at handling and conceptualizing shapes, then they may respond to teaching sounds through the shape of the mouth.

Right-brained children often are able to pick up sounds through the visual information of the shape of the mouth. For instance, an "m" is formed by placing the lips tightly together in a horizontal plane. No sound needs to come out of the mouth in order for the child to be able to distinguish that when the lips are put this way, it is the sound of "m." They begin to distinguish sounds by the feel of their lips and tongue and by the shape of their mouth while forming the sounds. This is a method that often is used in teaching a deaf child to speak. There are many picture cards on the market showing the correct positions. A speech therapist will have catalogues to order from.

# DOMINOES AND DICE

Some children can relate the symbols for numerals to dot patterns more easily than to objects they can count. Use dominoes or dice. Have the children memorize the dot pattern for each numeral.

EXAMPLE:

$$\boxed{\,\bullet\,} = 1 \qquad \boxed{\begin{smallmatrix}\bullet\ \ \bullet\\[2pt]\bullet\ \ \bullet\end{smallmatrix}} = 4$$

Once they have memorized the pattern, give them dominoes or pairs of dice and have them write the problems they see. Have them see how many different problems they can make using only two dominoes or one pair of dice.

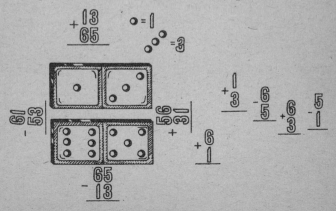

$$\begin{array}{r} 13 \\ +65 \\ \hline \end{array}$$

$$\circ = 1$$

$$\overset{\circ}{\underset{\circ\ \circ}{}} = 3$$

$$\begin{array}{r} 1 \\ +3 \\ \hline \end{array} \qquad \begin{array}{r} 6 \\ -5 \\ \hline \end{array} \qquad \begin{array}{r} 6 \\ +3 \\ \hline \end{array} \qquad \begin{array}{r} 5 \\ -1 \\ \hline \end{array}$$

$$\begin{array}{r} 61 \\ -53 \\ \hline \end{array} \qquad \begin{array}{r} 56 \\ 31 \\ \hline + \end{array} \qquad \begin{array}{r} 6 \\ +1 \\ \hline \end{array}$$

$$\begin{array}{r} 65 \\ -13 \\ \hline \end{array}$$

147

# HELPING VERBS

One of the most difficult abstract concepts to teach children is when to use a helping verb. I have found that through the use of an absurdity the children learn the practical application very quickly.

For example:
1. For two verbs that are the same length, such as "went" and "gone," create an absurdity such as "the verb with the hole shot in it takes the helper because it needs help getting to the hospital."
2. If the two verbs are not the same length, such as "be" and "been," you might say "the taller one takes the helper because he is so tall he needs help standing up."

# MUSIC

Many right-brained children have a great affinity for music and rhythm. They are able to listen to music and have it affect them emotionally, have it change their mood or behavior. They can move into the rhythm of the music and allow it to work for them.

Many parents and teachers find that when the right-brained child does his homework while music is playing he completes it sooner and often makes fewer errors. It also is true that when soft music, especially music at 4-4 time, is played while children are learning new material, not only is information they already have received stabilized but they also are able to think better and their focus of attention appears to be longer than most children's.

The book, *Superlearning,* by Ostrander and Schroeder, goes into greater detail on the research that has been done in this area and the methods used in this type of teaching. The approach is effective not only for the younger child but also for persons of any age.

# MOVEMENT AND MUSIC

Many right-brained children have a natural affinity for movement in music. These are the children who are continuously beating a rhythm on their desks with their pencils, moving in rhythm down the hall or while they are trying to eat supper, or dancing in one form or another whenever they hear any kind of music.

These also are the children who learn better by combining movement and music rather than by doing motor movement alone. Simply combine any kind of movement with singing matched to what you are teaching; put what you are teaching into a familiar song; or play music simultaneously with the learning act. To teach syllables, you may have the child sing the syllables, with the first syllable on a high note and the second syllable on a low note, tapping the pencil with the singing. To teach arithmetic, you may have the children sing the addition facts or times tables while they put a motor movement such as a clap or clicking of the fingers to each number.

# SINGING SPELLING WORDS

Older children sometimes do not want to do their spelling words by using jumping jacks, by writing them in the air, or by doing the various other activities that already have been mentioned for teaching spelling words. These same children often are willing to sing their spelling words, either to a song that they already know or simply to the scale. Once this method is taught, the older child can do this singing internally, while the younger child can do it as a group in the classroom under teacher direction or at home with his parents while working on spelling words. Singing spelling words is simply another way of taking one of the right-hemispheric talents and connecting it to one of the left-hemispheric tasks that may be difficult for the child.

When children were asked to read orally in the one-room school houses, they read as total group rather than individually. When children read as a total group, it is called choral reading. What seems to happen is that they fall into a rhythmic chanting pattern that taps the capabilities in the right hemisphere. In working with children, I have found that allowing them to read orally as a group over a short period of time greatly increases their oral reading and removes the stress they feel when having to read individually in front of the other children. While they are reading together, the story can be recorded so that the child who needs more reinforcement can listen to it while following the book, enabling the parent or teacher to be occupied with other tasks while the child is working individually.

"When I outgrow my names
and facts and theories
or when reality leaves
them behind, I become dead
if I don't go on to new
ways of seeing things."
—Hugh Prather

# 4

# One Step
# Beyond

Since I started this book, my ideas have
changed or, rather, expanded. I still believe in
hemispheric specialization and the part it plays
in education. I still believe that alternative
methods of teaching that use color, movement,
imagery, and a whole-to-part approach enable
many children to learn more quickly and easily. But new doors are opening. Ideas such as
the triune brain, cognitive growth spurts, and
a consciousness that exists beyond our concepts will enable us to gain a deeper understanding of learning, which will open doors to
new approaches.

We will begin to understand how the two
hemispheres work together to give the individual a holistic view of his natural environment.
If either hemisphere is limited in its processing
ability, the picture is not whole and the indi-

vidual's perspective is limited. As out understanding grows, new methods and refinements will be added to those that appear in this book. We will begin to develop methods to strengthen the right hemisphere of those who are very left-hemispheric. Finally, we will understand how to balance the two hemispheres and reach for our highest human potential. This potential is achieved when both hemispheres are working to their capacity and the information from both is integrated into a whole.

This integration creates an intelligence far greater than the sum of its parts. It is an intelligence that exists beyond specialization and beyond the individual modes of processing present in each hemisphere. It is this intelligence that is the unknown. It is the intelligence that invents, creates, and evolves. We may never understand this elusive concept, but we must keep trying. We must give children of the world a chance to reach their greatest heights!

# HEMISPHERIC SPECIALIZATION AND BRAIN FUNCTION

## BOOKS

Ayres, A.J., *Sensory Integration and Learning,* Los Angeles, Western Psych., 1972.

Bandler, Richard, *Frogs Into Princes,* Moab, Utah, Real People Press, 1979.

Blakemore, Colin, *Mechanics of the Mind,* Cambridge, Cambridge University Press, 1977.

Blakeslee, Thomas, *Right Brain,* Garden City, Doubleday, 1980.

Bruner, Jerome S., *Beyond the Information Given,* New York, W.W. Norton and Co., 1973.

Bruner, Jerome S., *On Knowing,* New York, Atheneum, 1973.

Buzan, Tony, *Use Both Sides of Your Brain,* New York, Dutton, 1974.

deQuiros, Julio B. & Schrager, Orlando L., *Neuropsychological Fundamentals in Learning Disabilities,* Novato, Calif., Academic Therapy Pub., 1978.

Dimond, S.J. and Beaumont, J.O., *Hemisphere Function in the Human Brain,* New York, Wiley, 1974.

Edwards B., *Drawing on the Right Side of the Brain. A Course in Enhancing Creativity and Artistic Confidence,* Los Angeles, J.P. Tarcher, Inc., 1979.

Fadely, Jack and Hosler, Virginia, *Understanding the Alpha Child at Home and School, Left and Right Hemispheric Function in Relation to Personality and Learning,* Springfield, Illinois, Charles C. Thomas, 1979.

Feldenkrais, Moshe, *Body and Mature Behavior,* New York, N.Y., International Universities Press, Inc., 1949.

Feldenkrais, Moshe, *The Case of Nora,* New York, Harper & Row, 1977.

Ferguson, Marilyn, *The Brain Revolution,* Taplinger Publishing Co., 1973.

Fox, Patricia L., *Reading as a Whole Brain Function,* The Reading Teacher, October, 1979.

Gaddes, William H., *Learning Disabilities and Brain Function,* New York, Springer-Verlag, 1980.

Gazzaniga, Michael S., *The Bisected Brain,* New York, Appleton-Century-Crofts, 1970.

Gazzaniga, Michael and LeDoux, Joseph E., *The Integrated Mind,* New York, Plenum Press, 1978.

Geschwind, Norman, *Language and the Brain,* Scientific American, April, 1972.

Gesell, Arnold, Ilg, Frances L. and Ames, Louise Bates, *The Child From Five to Ten,* New York, Harper and Row, 1977.

Goldberg, Hermand K. and Schiffman, Gilbert B., *Dyslexia—Problems of Reading Disabilities,* New York, Grune & Stratton, 1972.

Grady, Michael P. and Luecke, Emily A., *Education and the Brain,* Phi Delta Kappa, 1978.

Gregory, R.L., *Eye and Brain,* McGraw-Hill, New York, 1974.

Hart, Leslie A., *How the Brain Works: A New Understanding of Human Learning, Emotion and Thinking,* New York Basic Books, Inc., 1975.

Hubel, David H. and others, *The Brain,* A Scientific American Book, San Francisco, W.H. Freeman and Co., 1979.

Kail, Robert, *The Development of Memory in Children,* San Francisco, W.H. Freeman and Co., 1979.

Kelley, E.C., *Education for What is Real,* New York, Harper, 1947.

Leonard, George B., *Education and Ecstasy,* New York, Dell, 1968.

Luria, A.R., *The Working Brain,* New York, Basic Books, Inc., 1973.

Montessori, Maria, *The Absorbant Mind,* New York, Dell Publishing Company, 1967.

Montessori, Maria, *The Discovery of the Child,* Notre Dame, Indiana, Fides Publishers, 1967.

Montessori, Maria, *The Secret of Childhood,* Madras, India; Orient Longman, Ltd., 1936.

Ornstein, Robert E.; Lee, Philip R.; Galin, David; Deikman, Arthur; Tart, Charles T., *Symposium on Consciousness,* Penguin Books, 1976.

Ornstein, Robert E., *The Nature of Human Consciousness,* San Francisco, W.H. Freeman and Co., 1973.

Ornstein, R.E., *Mind Field,* New York, Grossman, 1976.

Ornstein, Robert E., *The Psychology of Consciousness,* San Francisco, W.H. Freeman, 1972.

Ostrander, S. and Schroeder, L., *Superlearning,* New York, Delacorte Press and the Confucian Press, 1979.

Paivio, Allen, *Imagery and Verbal Processes,* New York, Holt, Rinehart and Winston, 1971.

Pearce, Joseph Chilton, *Exploring the Crack in the Cosmic Egg,* New York, Julian Press, 1974.

Pelletier, K. and Garfield, C., *Consciousness East and West,* New York, Harper & Row, 1976.

Penfield, W. and Lamar, R., *Speech and Brain Mechanisms,* Princeton, N.J., Princeton Univ. Press, 1959.

Penfield, Wilder, *The Mystery of the Mind,* Princeton, N.J., Princeton Univ. Press, 1975.

Piaget, J. & Inhelder, B., *Memory and Intelligence,* New York, Basic Books, 1973.

160

Piaget, Jean, *To Understand Is to Invent,* New York, Grossman, 1973.

Pines, Maya, *The Brain Changers,* New York, Signet, 1973.

Prather, Hugh, *Notes to Myself,* Moab, Utah, Real People Press, 1979, New York, Bantam, 1976.

Read, Herbert, *Education Through Art,* Pantheon, 1958, 1974.

Restak, R.M., *The Brain: The Last Frontier,* Garden City, New York, Doubleday, 1979.

Rose, Steven, *The Conscious Brain,* New York, Vintage Books, 1976.

Sagan, Carl, *The Dragons of Eden,* New York, Random House, 1977.

Samples, Bob, *The Metaphoric Mind,* Reading, Massachusetts, Addison-Wesley, 1976.

Segalowitz, S. and Gruber, F., *Language Development and Neurological Theory,* New York, Academic Press, 1977.

Silverstein, Alvin and Virginia B., *The Left-Handers World,* New York, Follett Publishing Co., 1977.

Standing, E.E., *The Montessori Revolution in Education,* New York, Random House, 1968.

Springer, Sally and Deutsch, George, *Left Brain, Right Brain,* San Francisco, W.H. Freeman and Company, 1981.

Tarnopol, Lester and Muriel, *Brain Function and Reading Disabilities,* Baltimore, University Park Press, 1977.

Thie, John F., *Touch for Health,* Marina Del Rey, Calif., DeVorss & Co., 1973.

Virshup, Evelyn, *Art and the Right Hemisphere,* Art Education, 1976.

Vygotsky, L.S., *Thought and Language,* Cambridge, Massachusetts, The M.I.T. Press, 1962.

Wittrock, M.C. and others, *The Human Brain,* Englewood Cliffs, New Jersey, Prentice-Hall, Inc., 1977.

# JOURNAL ARTICLES

Bakan, Paul. 1976. "The Right Brain is the Dreamer." *Psychology Today,* November 1976, p. 66–68.

Bakan, Paul. 1969. "Hypnotizability, Laterality of Eye-Movements and Functional Brain Asymmetry." *Perceptual and Motor Skills,* 28:927–32.

Bakan, Paul. 1971. "The Eyes Have It." *Psychology Today,* April 1971, 4(11):64–67.

Bakker, D., Smink, T. and Reitsma, P. 1973. "Early Dominance and Reading Ability." *Cortex,* 9:302–12.

Beaumont, J.G. 1976. "The Cerebral Laterality of 'Minimal Brain Damage' Children." *Cortex,* 12:373–82.

Beckman, Lucile. 1977. "The Use of the Block Design Sub Test of the WISC as an Identifying Instrument for Spatial Children." *Gifted Child Quarterly,* Spring 1977.

Bever, T. and Chiarello, R. 1974. "Cerebral Dominance in Musicians and Nonmusicians." *Science,* 185:537–39.

Brandwein, P. and Orstein, R. 1977. "The Duality of the Mind." *Instructor,* January 1977, Volume LXXXVI, Number 5, p. 54–58.

Brazier, M.A. 1962. "The Analysis of Brain Waves." *Scientific American,* June 1962.

Botkin, A., Schmaltz, L. and Lamb, D. 1977. "'Overloading' the Left Hemisphere in Right-handed Subjects with Verbal and Motor Tasks." *Neuropsychologia,* 15:591–96.

Buck, Craig. 1976. "Knowing the Left from the Right." *Human Behavior,* June 1976, p. 29–35.

Dacey, Rob. 1975. "Inside the Brain: The Last Great Frontier." *Saturday Review,* August 9, 1975, p. 13.

Damasio, H., Damasio, A., Castro-Caldas, A. and Ferro, J.M. 1976. "Dichotic Listening Pattern in Relation to Interhemispheric Disconnexion." *Neuropsychologia,* 14:247–50.

DeRenzi, E., Faglioni, P. and Previdi, P. 1977. "Spatial Memory and Hemispheric Locus of Lesion." *Cortex,* 13:124–29.

Foster, Suzanne. 1977. "Hemisphere Dominance and the Art Process." *Art Education,* February 1977, p. 28–29.

Franco, L., and R. W. Sperry. 1977(b). "Hemisphere Lateralization for Cognitive Processing of Geometry." *Neuropsychologia,* 15:107–14.

Garrett, Susan V. 1976. "Putting Our Whole Brain to Use: A Fresh Look at the Creative Process." *J. Creat. Behav.,* 10(4): 239–49.

Gazzaniga, Michael S. 1967. "The Split Brain in Man." *Brain and Consciousness,* August, 1967, p. 118–23.

Gazzaniga, Michael S. 1972. "One Brain—Two Minds?" *American Scientist,* May-June 1972, p. 311–17.

Gazzaniga, Michael S. 1975. "Review of the Split Brain." *J. Neurology,* 209:75–79.

Gott, Peggy S. 1973(b). "Cognitive Abilities Following Right and Left Hemispherectomy." *Cortex,* 9:266–73.

Gross, Yigal, R. Franko and I. Lewin. 1978. "Effects of Voluntary Eye Movements on Hemispheric Activity and Choice of Cognitive Mode." *Neuropsychologia,* 16·653–55.

Gur, R.E., R.C. Gur, and L. Harris. 1975(a). "Cerebral Activation, as Measured by Subjects' Lateral Eye Movements, Is Influenced by Experimenter Location." *Neuropsychologia,* 13:35–44.

Gur, R.E., and R.C. Gur. 1977(b). "Sex Differences in the Relations Among Handedness, Sighting-Dominance and Eye-Acuity." *Neuropsychologia,* 15:585–90.

Guyer, B. LaRue and Morton P. Friedman. 1975. "Hemispheric Processing and Cognitive Styles in Learning-Disabled and Normal Children." *Child Development,* September 1975, Volume 46, Number 3, p. 658–668.

Haber, Ralph Norman. 1979. "How We Remember What We See." *Scientific American,* 222(5):104–12.

Hart, Leslie A. 1981. "The Three-Brain Concept and the Classroom." *Phi Delta Kappa,* March 1981, Volume 62, Number 7, p. 504–506.

Hecaen, J., and J. Sauguet. 1971. "Cerebral Dominance in Left-Handed Subjects." *Cortex,* 7:19–48.

Hellige, J., and P. Cox. 1976. "Effects of Concurrent Verbal Memory on Recognition of Stimuli from the Left and Right Visual Fields." *J. Exper. Psych.*, 2(2):210–21.

Hunter, Madeline. 1977. "Right-Brained Kids in Left-Brained Schools." *The Education Digest*, February 1977, p. 8–10.

Ingvar, David H. and Martin S. Schwartz. 1975. "Brain Blood Flow." *Journal of Learning Disabilities*, February 1975, Volume 8, Number 2, p. 26–27.

Kershner, J., and A. Jeng. 1972. "Dual Functional Hemispheric Asymmetry in Visual Perception: Effects of Ocular Dominance and Post-exposural Processes." *Neuropsychologia*, 10:437–45.

Kershner, John R. 1975. "Reading and Laterality Revisited." *J. Spec. Ed.*, 9(3):269–79.

Kershner, John R. 1977(b). "Cerebral Dominance in Disabled Readers, Good Readers, and Gifted Children: Search for a Valid Model." *Child Development*, 48:61–67.

Kimura, Doreen. 1973(a). "The Asymmetry of the Human Brain." *Scientific American*, March 1973, p. 70–78.

Lake, D., and M. Bryden. 1976. "Handedness and Sex Differences in Hemispheric Asymmetry." *Brain and Language*, 3:266–82.

Lansdell, H. 1964. "Sex Differences in Hemispheric Asymmetries of the Human Brain." *Nature*, 203-(4944):550.

Lomas, J. and D. Kumura. 1976. "Intrahemispheric Interaction Between Speaking and Sequential Manual Activity." *Neuropsychologia,* 14:23–33.

Luria, A.R. and E.G. Simernitskaya. 1977. "Interhemispheric Relations and the Functions of the Minor Hemisphere." *Neuropsychologia,* 15:175–78.

Marcel, T., L. Katz, and M. Smith. 1974. "Laterality and Reading Proficiency." *Neuropsychologia,* 12: 131–39.

Marshall, John C. 1973. "Some Problems and Paradoxes Associated with Recent Accounts of Hemispheric Specialization." *Neuropsychologia,* 11:463–70.

McFarland, K., M.L. McFarland, J.D. Bain, and R. Ashton. 1978. "Ear Differences of Abstract and Concrete Word Recognition." *Neuropsychologia, 16:* 555–61.

McNamara, B.E. 1980. "Implications of Research on Metamemory." *Academic Therapy,* 1980, 16:133–137.

McNeil, Malcolm R., and C.E. Hamre. 1974. "A Review of Measures of Lateralized Cerebral Hemispheric Functions." *J. Learning Disabilities,* 7(6): 51–59.

McGlone, J., and W. Davidson. 1973(a). "The Relationship Between Cerebral Speech Laterality and Spatial Ability with Special Reference to Sex and Hand Preference." *Neuropsychologia,* 11:105–13.

McGlone, J., and A. Kertesz. 1973(b). "Sex Differences in Cerebral Processing of Visuospatial Tasks." *Cortex,* 9:313–20.

McGlone, Jeannette. 1978. "Sex Differences in Functional Brain Asymmetry." *Cortex,* 14:122–28.

Miller, Edgar. 1971. "Handedness and the Pattern of Human Ability." *Br. J. Psychol.,* 62(1):111–12.

Molfese, Dennis L. 1977. "Infant Cerebral Asymmetry." In *Language Development and Neurological Theory.* S. Segalowitz and F. Gruber, eds. New York: Academic Press.

Moore, W.H., Jr. 1976. "Bilateral Tachistoscopic Word Perception of Stutterers and Normal Subjects." *Brain and Language,* 3:434–43.

Morais, Jose and Michele Landercy. 1977. "Listening to Speech While Retaining Music: What Happens to the Right-ear Advantage?" *Brain and Language,* 4:295–308.

Olson, Meredith B. 1977(b). "Right or Left Hemispheric Information Processing in Gifted Students." *The Gifted Child Quarterly,* 21(1):116–21.

Peterson, J., and L. Lansky, 1974. "Left-handedness Among Architects: Some Facts and Speculation." *Perceptual and Motor Skills,* 38:547–50.

Piaget, Jean. 1953. "How Children Form Mathematical Concepts." *Scientific American,* 189:74–79.

Pizzamiglio, L., and M. Cecchini. 1971. "Development of Hemispheric Dominance in Children from 5 to 10 Years of Age and Their Relations with the Development of Cognitive Processes." *Brain Research,* 31:361–78.

Ray, W., M. Morell, A. Frediani, and D. Tucker. 1976. "Sex Differences and Lateral Specialization of Hemispheric Functioning." *Neuropsychologia,* 14: 391–94.

Regelski, Thomas A. 1977. "Music Education and the Human Brain." *The Education Digest,* October 1977.

Rennels, Max R. 1976. "Cerebral Symmetry: An Urgent Concern for Education." *Phi Delta Kappan,* March 1976, Volume 57, Number 7, p. 471–472.

Rizzolatti, G., and H. Buchtel. 1977. "Hemispheric Superiority in Reaction Time to Faces: A Sex Difference." *Cortex,* 13:300–5.

Robbins, K., and D. McAdam, 1974. "Interhemispheric Alpha Asymmetry and Imagery Mode." *Brain and Language,* 1:189–93.

Sackeim, Harold and R. Gur. 1978. "Lateral Asymmetry in Intensity of Emotional Expression." *Neuropsychologia,* 16:473–81.

Sage, Wayne. 1976. "The Split Brain Lab." *Human Behavior,* June 1976, p. 25–28.

Saks, Judith Brody. 1979. "Latest Brain Research Offers Lessons in Learning." *The Executive Educator,* October 1979.

Samples, Bob. 1977. "Mind Cycles and Learning." *Phi Delta Kappan,* May 1977, p. 688–92.

Samples, Robert E. 1975. "Are You Teaching Only One Side of the Brain?" *Learning,* February 1975, p. 25–28.

Springer, S., and M. Gazzaniga. 1975. "Dichotic Testing of Partial and Complete Split Brain Subjects." *Neuropsychologia,* 13:341–46.

Sugishita, Morihiro. 1978. "Mental Association in the Minor Hemisphere of a Commissurotomy Patient." *Neuropsychologia,* 16:229–32.

Thomson, M.E. 1976. "A Comparison of Laterality Effects in Dyslexics and Controls Using Verbal Dichotic Listening Tasks." *Neuropsychologia.*

Tucker, D., R. Roth, B. Arneson, and V. Buckingham. 1977. "Right Hemisphere Activation During Stress." *Neuropsychologia,* 15:697–700.

Walkup, Lewis E. 1965. "Creativity in Science Through Visualization." *Perceptual and Motor Skills,* 21:35–41.

Witelson, Sandra. 1976. "Sex and the Single Hemisphere: Specialization of the Right Hemisphere for Spatial Processing." *Science,* 193:425–26.

Witelson, Sandra F. 1977(a). "Development Dyslexia: Two Right Hemispheres and None Left." *Science,* 195:309–11

Zaidel, Eran. 1976. "Auditory Vocabulary of the Right Hemisphere Following Brain Bisection or Hemidecortication." *Cortex,* 12:191–211.

Zaidel, Eran. 1977. "Unilateral Auditory Language Comprehension on the Token Test Following Cerebral Commissurotomy and Hemispherectomy." *Neuropsychologia,* 15:1–18.

# LEARNING STRATEGIES

Axline, Virginia, *Dibs in Search of Self,* Ballantine Books, New York, 1964.

Berg, Leila, *Reading and Loving,* Routledge and Kegan Paul, London and Boston, 1977.

Brown, Rosellen; Hoffman, Marvin; Kushner, Martin; Lopate, Phillip; and Murphy, Sheila, *The Whole Word,* New York, Teachers & Writers, 1972.

Canfield, Jack and Wells, Harold C., *100 Ways to Enhance Self-Concept in the Classroom,* New Jersey, Prentice-Hall, 1976.

Chappel, Bernice M., *A Time for Learning,* Ann Arbor Publishers, Inc., Worthington, Ohio, 1974.

Curwin, Richard L. and Curwin, Geri, *Developing Individual Values in the Classroom,* Learning Handbooks, 1974.

DeMille, Richard, *Put Your Mother on the Ceiling,* New York, N.Y., Penguin Books, 1967.

Diskin, Eve, *Yoga For Children,* Warner Communications Co., 1976.

Fadimon, James, *Transpersonal Education,* Prentice-Hall, Inc., New Jersey, 1976.

Fadely, Jack and Hosler, Virginia, *Understanding the Alpha Child at Home and School,* Springfield, Ill., Charles C. Thomas, 1979.

Feldenkrais, Moshe, *Awareness Through Movement,* New York, Harper & Row, 1972.

Fischer, Charlotte and Hamilton, Hales, *Planning Discovery Investigations,* Bellevue, Washington, Discovery Learning, 1978.

Forte, Imogene and MacKenzie, Joy, *Days of Wonder*—Teachers Edition, Nashville, Incentive Publications, 1978.

Furth and Wachs, *Thinking Goes to School,* Oxford University Press, 1974.

Fynn, *Mister God This is Anna,* Ballantine Books, New York, 1974.

Getman, G.N., *How to Develop Your Child's Intelligence,* Luverne, Minn., 1962.

Hendricks, G. and R. Wills, *The Centering Book,* Englewood Cliffs, N.J., Prentice-Hall, 1975.

Hirsch, Elizabeth S., *The Block Book,* National Association for the Education of Young Children, Washington, D.C., 1974.

Johnson, Doris J. and Myklebust, Helmer K., *Learning Disabilities Educational Principles and Practice,* New York, Grune & Stratton, 1967.

Kaufman, Barry Neil, *Son Rise,* Warner Books, 1976.

Lorton, Mary Baratta, *Mathematics Their Way,* Menlo Park, Calif., Addison-Wesley, 1976.

Lorton, Mary Baratta, *Workjobs,* Menlo Park, Calif., 1975.

Lupin, Mimi, *Peace, Harmony, Awareness*, Massachusetts, Teaching Resources, 1977.

Maid, Amy and Wallace, Roger, *Not Just Schoolwork*, Amherst, Mass., Mandala, 1976.

Marzollo, Jean and Lloyd, Janice, *Learning Through Play*, Harper and Row, 1972.

Medvedeff, Eugene, *New Dimensions in Learning*, Westinghouse Learning Corp., 1975.

Medvedeff, Eugene and Dearth, Beverly, *New Dimensions in Learning, Prescriptive Educational Systems*, Akron, Ohio, 1969.

Michaelis, Bill and Dolores, *Noncompetitive Activities and Play*, Learning Handbooks, 1977.

Miller, Maureen, *To Share with Your Children*, Argus Communications, 1978.

Murphy, Richard, *Imaginary Worlds*, New York, Teachers & Writers, 1974.

Ostrander, Sheila, and L. Schroeder, *Superlearning*, New York, Pocketbook, 1975.

Peck, Judith, *Leap to the Sun*, New Jersey, Prentice-Hall, 1979.

Rubin, Theodore Isaac, *Jordi, Lisa and David*, New York, Ballantine Books, 1960, 1961.

Simon, Sidney, *Caring, Feelings, Touching*, Argus Communications, Niles, Illinois, 1976.

Smith, Adam, *Powers of Mind*, New York, Random House, 1975.

Sokolov, A.M., *Inner Speech and Thought,* New York, Plenum Press, 1972.

Staley, Frederick A., *Outdoor Education for the Whole Child,* Dubuque, Iowa, Kendall/Hunt Pub. Co., 1979.

Stanish, Bob, *I Believe in Unicorns,* Illinois, Good Apple, Inc., 1979.

Wedemeyer, Avaril and Cejka, Joyce, *Learning Games for Exceptional Children,* Love Publishing Co., Denver, Colorado, 1971.

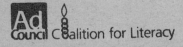